BUILDING THE
HIGH-PERFORMANCE
SALES
FORCE

BUILDING THE
HIGH-PERFORMANCE
SALES
FORCE

JOE PETRONE

American Management Association

New York • Atlanta • Boston • Chicago • Kansas City • San Francisco • Washington, D.C.
Brussels • Mexico City • Tokyo • Toronto

Library of Congress Cataloging-in-Publication Data

Petrone, Joe.
    Building the high-performance sales force / Joe Petrone.
        p.   cm.
    Includes bibliographical references and index.
    ISBN 0-8144-0219-4
    1. Sales management. 2. Total quality management. I. Title.
    HF5438.4.P47   1994
    658.3'044—dc20   93-43676
                                                                      CIP

Printing number

10   9   8   7   6   5   4   3   2   1

Contents

Chapter 6. Total Quality Selling 111

• *Trust and Empathy: Keys to Quality in Sales* • *Continuous Improvement* • *Four Cultural Elements Required for Total Quality Selling* • *Case Studies: Implementing Quality in the Sales Organization*

Chapter 7. The Customer-Focused Selling Process 157

• *Sales-Driven vs. Customer-Focused Selling* • *Steps in the Selling Process* • *Customer-Focused Selling: Model of the Future*

Chapter 8. The 120-Day Plan 179

• *The First Thirty Days* • *The First Sixty Days* • *The First Ninety Days* • *The First 120 Days*

Index 201

Preface

The field of sales and sales management is changing rapidly. Today, sales managers and salespeople in virtually every industry are being pressured to generate more revenues with less support in the face of increasing competition and, in many cases, shrinking markets.

Some sales managers are being given responsibility for managing larger sales teams, as their companies downsize and consolidate sales districts and regions. Others are absorbing the marketing function, as their companies attempt to cut costs. All are struggling to meet senior management's demand for short-term profits while satisfying the demands of sales reps for long-term professional development. It's a tough balancing act.

In this environment, typical approaches to sales and sales management won't work. The successful sales manager in the 1990s will be the one who boldly confronts the status quo, who understands the unique challenges of selling in a competitive climate of constant change, who adopts new strategies and leadership principles to meet these challenges.

Unfortunately, no book currently on the market addresses the rapidly changing roles and responsibilities of today's salespeople and sales managers. That's why I decided to write this one. *Building the High-Performance Sales Force* provides an insider's perspective on how sales managers and salespeople can meet the serious challenges they'll face in the coming decade, from squeezing more revenue out of increasingly competitive markets to implementing Total Quality Selling.

Chapter 1 provides an overview of the environment in which sales managers will operate. Each of the following six chapters (2–7) focuses on a specific challenge for sales managers in the 1990s. These chapters show salespeople and sales managers how to do more with less, how to thrive in the midst of change, and how to generate sustained productivity, not just by working harder but also by working smarter. Readers are shown how to:

- Boost salespeople's productivity and enhance their loyalty
- Teach sales reps to become more self-managing
- Implement a Progressive Goal Management system that links individual goals to corporate performance
- Apply micro and macro management tools to maximize sales performance
- Use the computer as an analytical tool for improving territory management and boosting sales productivity, in addition to the common reporting and communications uses
- Methodically pinpoint the causes of substandard performance so they can be quickly corrected
- Grow sales, even in a highly competitive marketplace
- Implement Total Quality Selling in order to gain a competitive edge

The last chapter presents a 120-day plan that the novice or veteran manager can use at any time to improve his or her effectiveness and enhance the performance of the sales force.

Building the High-Performance Sales Force is filled with anecdotes and real life examples drawn from my own extensive experience and that of dozens of other sales managers and salespeople. It includes models and strategies that can be easily adopted by any organization. Taken together, the chapters provide a winning game plan for managing sales in turbulent economic times. I know it's a winning plan because the players—my own team of salespeople and others like them—are beating the odds, achieving record sales in recessionary times.

Many people have contributed to the development of this book. My thanks to all of the sales managers and salespeople whose stories are told in these pages. I would like to acknowledge the contribution of Jeannine Drew, whose insights and editing skills significantly improved the content and quality of the manuscript. I also wish to thank my editor at AMACOM, Andrea Pedolsky, who provided guidance and support throughout the project.

This book could not have been produced without the support and understanding of my wife, Deborah, and the encouragement of my managers, Roland Pampel, Bob Terrio, and Bruce Ross.

Chapter 1

A New Era in Sales Management

The sales manager in the 1990s faces a number of difficult challenges. Salespeople, disillusioned by layoffs and limited job opportunities, have become distrustful of management and disloyal to their employers. Domestic and international competition is intensifying. Resources are becoming increasingly scarce. Because of rampant downsizing, sales managers are being forced to take on more and more responsibility. Shareholders are demanding immediate profits. Customers are demanding higher quality and better service. Job security, for sales managers and salespeople, is a thing of the past.

How did we get into this predicament? To understand the sales environment of the 1990s, it is helpful to trace the evolution of the sales organization during the decade of the 1980s.

The Extravagant Eighties

The 1980s were a heady time for salespeople, the primary generators of revenue. As long as they worked hard and were considered loyal, their sales jobs were secure.

There was safety in being part of a large national sales force. We knew that the overperformance of some salespeople would balance out the underperformers. So what if Anne in Milwaukee had a bad year? John in Houston or Mike in New York City would more than make up for it. As long as the company was growing as a whole, the environment was hospitable to salespeople, productive and unproductive alike.

Revenue growth rates of as much as 20 percent were common in my industry (scientific instruments) and many others during the 1980s, making the sales environment friendly indeed. But these high rates of growth often hid excessive operating expenses for lavish sales meetings, awards banquets, and new product introductions at fancy resorts. Money seemed to be no object.

Growing Competition

In companies on the fast track of growth in the 1980s, expenses were not closely scrutinized by upper management. But they were carefully watched by small, cost-conscious, entrepreneurial firms, who took advantage of the bloated expense accounts of large companies to enter their markets and win their business. They began offering lower prices for products that were equivalent, if not superior to, those of the large firms.

These lower priced competitors convinced many customers that the "customized" offerings and "proprietary" products of Fortune 500 companies were really no better than their own, less expensive products. Customer loyalty to the big firms began to decline. The days of padding profits were clearly coming to an end.

The end was hastened by advances in technology, which turned many proprietary products into commodities virtually overnight. The computer industry is a good example. Over the past decade, PC clones with the same performance levels as name brands, but with lower price tags, have become more popular than the big names. "Nobody ever got fired for choosing IBM" was a refrain commonly heard in my industry and many others during the 1980s. You don't hear it anymore.

As manufacturing technology improved, small manufacturers began turning out even high quality products. The reliability of these new generation products made the product support issue diminish in importance. Increasingly it was clear that the only thing that separated large companies from small ones was price.

The result was that in many parts of the manufacturing sector, cost-conscious competitors and an increasingly savvy customer base forced large companies to lower their prices. To maintain their profits, they would have to find ways of lowering their costs. The quickest way was to lay off workers.

Downsizing the Sales Force

To reduce operating costs, many businesses began to shut down inefficient plants and consolidate them with other facilities. Some large companies moved to Mexico to take advantage of cheaper labor costs. Many began to subcontract work to overseas sources.

To compensate for declining prices and profit margins, some firms began to look for more cost-effective distribution strategies. In many cases, that meant eliminating or reducing the direct sales force.

To remain competitive, one plastics manufacturer began to substitute brokers for direct salespeople. The brokers would be given an exclusive on all accounts of less than $100,000. This enabled the firm to pass on a lower price to the broker, who would buy in large volume and have lower selling expenses than the direct salesperson. Many sales reps lost their jobs as a result of this change in strategy.

Other industries pursued similar strategies. Early in 1992, Apple Computer took its business development managers, whose job was to search out new strategic markets, and turned them into sales reps. The company also began distributing its products through four retail store chains: Sears, Circuit City, Montgomery Ward, and BizMart.

Takeover Mania

Large companies that didn't cut their costs became targets for takeovers. In the mid-1980s, corporate raiders and venture capitalists began executing highly leveraged buyouts of midsize and large companies that were struggling under the burden of increased competition. They raised much of their money by promising that the companies, once acquired, would return to profitability within a year.

The strategy they used to hit their profitability goals was to strip unprofitable operations from the company and lay off workers. Whatever long-term negative effect this may have had on the companies, the short-term savings went directly to the bottom line.

Even companies that weren't bought out were affected by the takeover mania in the 1980s. The constant threat of acquisition enhanced the bias of U.S. companies toward generating short-term profits, usually by decreasing expenses in ways that directly or indirectly resulted in layoffs.

Job Insecurity

Throughout the economy, salespeople began to wonder: Will I still have a job in two or three years? In many cases, the answer was no. There was a gradual decline in direct sales positions in the 1980s, especially in mature industries, and continued reductions can be expected in the 1990s. For the salesperson as well as other employees, job security has become a thing of the past.

When I signed on with my first company right out of college, I expected to be there my entire career. A great number of secretaries, salespeople, and managers had been with the company for more than thirty years. Company pins and anniversary dinners were a regular feature of corporate life. The company was the employees' home away from home, and colleagues were like a second family.

As a sales manager in the late 1980s, when I recruited a new hire, the first thing I looked at was the length of time the candidate had spent with previous employers. Sales managers expected a minimum of three, and preferably five, years in previous positions. Anything less than a five-year track record was viewed by me and other managers as job-hopping. We wanted salespeople who would stay with our companies for years.

Once they were hired, the good performers would see rapid promotions to new positions. It was not uncommon for a sales rep to be given three promotions within a three-year period, from an associate sales representative to a management position.

If someone's sales performance was not good but he was a hard worker, the company would try to find him another position within the firm, such as purchasing agent or product specialist. Although this was viewed as a slap on the hand, the employee knew that the company would not terminate him.

Today, no one can *expect* to stay with the same firm for a lifetime. People can now expect to have multiple jobs with a number of companies.

In the mid- to late 1980s, employees regularly asked me if they could anticipate being laid off. This question is heard infrequently—if at all—today. Most employees seem to recognize that layoffs will be a fact of life for most companies in the foreseeable future.

In an ongoing survey of more than 500 managers, *Industry Week* asks whether the respondents are fairly confident they will be with their current employer five years from now. The number of respondents who say yes has been steadily declining. When the question was asked in 1970, 75 percent of middle and senior managers said they planned on being with their then current employer five years later. In a 1976 survey, the figure dropped to 70 percent; by 1983 it had fallen to 64 percent and by 1990, less than half of respondents—only 49 percent—said they planned on staying with their current employer for another five years.

Although the survey focused on managers, it's reasonable to assume that other employees, including salespeople, feel the same way. After a decade of sometimes ruthless downsizing, many salespeople look to a future of uncertainty and distrust.

The Trust Gap

As media attention to takeovers and acquisitions increased in the mid-1980s, employees began to worry about the possibility that their own company might be acquired next. And they began to question senior management about the possibility.

Many companies that were indeed targets for takeovers handled the situation badly. Instead of being open with their employees about the possibility of a takeover, senior management denied the possibility outright or fudged the issue. In response to repeated questioning, the CEO might make an impassioned statement: "There will be no takeover of this company. We are not for sale. If someone does try to acquire us, we will use state law and poison pills to protect us."

Such pronouncements were frequently followed by a takeover and subsequent layoff. The laid-off workers, and more importantly, those left behind, could only conclude that upper management had lied to them.

This lack of communication is one of the factors that has led to a growing trust gap between salespeople and their employers. Another factor is the unfairness of much of the downsizing of the past decade. In talking with my colleagues in other industries, it seems that in many cases politics, not performance, determines who gets fired and who gets to stay. Even if employees are not targeted for political reasons, they might be laid off arbitrarily just to fill a department's quota.

Such unfair layoffs lead to low morale, rumor spreading, lost productivity, and reduced trust. Survivors wonder, "Why should I put my faith in the company, when I might be fired tomorrow for no reason?" Employees who work hard and remain loyal to their employers when times are tough are especially bitter when they are laid off.

Whereas rank-and-file employees were exposed to the threat of layoffs in the wake of corporate takeovers, senior managers were usually protected, and this widened the trust gap. In the wake of corporate restructurings, senior managers were given golden parachutes. Huge perks of one year's pay plus stock options and continued health care coverage were frequently awarded to those lucky enough to be in senior management positions during a hostile takeover.

Meanwhile, the rest of the employee base, including sales reps and sales managers, received a few weeks' worth of severance pay if they were lucky and if they agreed to sign a release excluding the raider from any future litigation. This generated a great deal of resentment and widened the trust gap between employers and employees.

Profits vs. People

After a layoff, those left behind are usually burdened with additional work for no extra pay. When technical sales support people are laid off, field sales reps must take on their jobs as best they can. Support tasks that were previously done in headquarters are now performed in the field.

When a support person is laid off, the sales forecast for the person's product line usually remains the same. This serves to demotivate salespeople even further. They are now faced with selling a product they know will receive no product support.

When sales reps and support people live with the constant threat that they will be laid off or, if they stay behind, will be overworked, they adopt a "why should I care?" attitude. Some rebel by giving the company only a forty-hour week and no more.

Even when people are not laid off, it's clear that, despite the rhetoric about people being "our greatest asset," increased short-term profits usually come at the expense of employees. Either they are forced to work harder for the same pay, or they are given some other signal that the company is more interested in profits than people.

When a drug company was recently acquired, the parent company began stressing the need to improve return on assets. At the same time, it announced that the Human Resources Department of the acquired company would be merged with the smaller HR department of the parent. Employees don't have to be rocket scientists to figure out the company's priorities. They begin to wonder, "If the company doesn't care about me, why should I care about the company?"

Employees become passive. They become conservative in their actions; they don't want to rock the boat. Or they become bitter and withdraw, doing the minimum they can to get by.

This is the challenging environment facing the sales manager of the 1990s.

The Renaissance Sales Manager

This challenging new era, in which companies must do more with less, in which the future is uncertain, jobs insecure, and salespeople have ample reason to be wary, calls for a new breed of sales manager. The tough-talking, intimidating sales manager of the past, who ruled by fear and threats, is an obsolete model for the 1990s. Today's sales manager must be tough but humane, cost-conscious but people-oriented. He or she must be capable of maintaining a delicate balance between the profit goals of the corporation and the personal needs of employees, while juggling a host of competing responsibilities, from developing an effective compensation plan to implementing a Total Quality Selling program to finding creative ways to generate more business with fewer salespeople.

This book provides all of the tools needed to become a "renaissance sales manager." It shows how to increase profits while developing people (Chapter 2). Chapter 3 discusses how to teach your salespeople to manage themselves, freeing up your time for other, more strategic responsibilities. Chapter 4 provides basic macro and micro management tools needed to direct the work of your sales force. Chapter 5 addresses the difficult challenge of increasing profits in a highly competitive marketplace. Chapters 6 and 7 show how to apply Total Quality concepts to your sales organization. Chapter 8 includes a step-by-step game plan that can be applied during the first four months in any sales management assignment, to get your sales force headed quickly in the right direction.

Sales management in the 1990s is far more complex than it was in past decades. But for those who understand and accept the challenges ahead and master the skills presented in the chapters ahead, the opportunities have never been greater.

Chapter 2

Developing People And Profits

The biggest challenge for the sales manager in the 1990s is to balance the company's goal of generating short-term profits with salespeople's needs for security and desire for fulfilling, financially rewarding work. This is no small challenge. It entails, among other things, defending the human needs of salespeople before numbers-oriented senior managers and eliciting high productivity from workers who may worry their jobs are in jeopardy. To be successful today, the sales manager must be skilled in human relations and savvy in financial management.

The Human Face of Sales Management

Creating a High Morale Environment

The attitude and morale of salespeople are more important to success than product knowledge and selling skills combined. In *Building a Winning Sales Force*, George Lumsden proposes the following equation:

$$\text{Skill} + \text{Knowledge} = \text{Competence};$$
$$\text{Competence} \times \text{Attitude} = \text{Performance}.[1]$$

I have applied this formula to my own sales force, and I find it works very well.

If a sales rep's attitude is poor, performance will be poor. However, if a rep's product knowledge is poor but his or her attitude is good, satisfactory performance is possible. For this reason, the sales manager's first job is to create an environment for positive attitudes and high morale.

One of the best ways to create a positive attitude/high morale sales environment is to take a genuine interest in employees. That means establishing a personal connection with your sales reps, not just a manager-subordinate relationship.

This doesn't mean you should become close friends with your reps, but that you should have some knowledge of their dreams and goals. You need to know what motivates them, what excites them, so you can use that information to help them transfer that energy and excitement to the workplace.

When I travel with my sales reps, I weave into the conversation questions focused on their own lives and interests. I do this in a conversational and genuinely interested manner. I am not trying to pry; I am simply looking for those components in their personal lives that directly relate to performance. I want to know what fires their imagination, what boosts their energy and inspires their commitment. My goal is to get them to pursue their jobs with the same level of enthusiasm and standards of excellence they apply to their favorite hobbies or other personal pursuits, by making connections between the two.

Your salespeople's personal lives are bound to impact their professional lives. One of my favorite Zen passages illustrates the interrelatedness of the various aspects of our lives:

> The master in the art of living makes little distinction between his work and his play, his labor and his leisure, his mind and his body, his education and his recreation, his love and his religion. He hardly knows which is which. He simply pursues his vision of excellence in whatever he does, leaving others to decide whether he is working or playing. To him he is always doing both.

My own experience confirms the wisdom of this Zen passage. Over the years, I've learned that excellence in sales comes not just from superior selling techniques but as a result of an attitude of excellence toward everything one does in life.

One of my salespeople and I reviewed his poor record of telephone cold calling. Paul's poor discipline in cold telephone calling led to consistent bad sales performance in his territory.

I sensed that Paul's discipline problem had to do with the fact that making cold calls is something most salespeople dread. So I tried to get him to see the task in a more positive light. I asked Paul if he was continuing to work out (I knew that he had joined a gym a while back). He said he was. I asked if he was working out consistently. He sheepishly replied no.

Paul was eager to become physically fit, so I focused the conversation in that direction. I agreed with him that working out, like making cold calls, is not much fun for most people, but I encouraged him to focus on the end result of all those workouts instead of concentrating on the workouts themselves. Now, Paul proudly states he rides the bicycle three times a week. More important, after I praised him in this area, Paul soon increased his telephone prospecting time from 10 percent to 45 percent. The results were dramatic: In Paul's second year with the company, his sales increased by 35 percent, as his self-discipline in working out spilled over to making cold calls.

Blending Work and Family

Being responsive to the personal side of your employees' lives is one of the most powerful ways to win their loyalty and boost their productivity, even in difficult situations. I learned this lesson from a sales manager of chemical adhesives. One of his sales reps, John, was asked to relocate from Salt lake City to Denver.

John had been unable to convince his wife to relocate. In trying to save his marriage and his job, he almost lost both.

The sales manager didn't realize his sales rep was having marital problems until he saw the mileage on John's van. Apparently, John's wife had not relocated to Colorado with her husband. She wanted to stay behind in their hometown of Salt Lake City and start a life beyond being a wife and mother. So John traveled home to Utah on weekends in an attempt to save the marriage.

However, Utah was not the location agreed upon for John's work; all of his customers were located at the opposite end of the territory in Colorado. John's excessive amount of time spent in the Salt Lake City area resulted in little activity in the pipeline.

It seemed the only way to help John blend work and family was to allow him to live in Salt Lake City. The sales manager and John spent several hours reviewing the anticipated business in his territory over the next two years. Since the territory covered a vast expanse of land, it was agreed that telephone coverage would be the most effective way to prospect. And it wouldn't matter whether John made those prospecting calls from Salt Lake City or Denver.

In the end, John was allowed to live in Salt Lake City. Soon after his permanent move back to his hometown, he captured the biggest order in his territory over the past seven years. Today, his family life is intact and his performance was record-breaking for his territory in the two most recent years.

Shielding the Sales Force

John's manager was more than accommodating to the unorthodox request to allow his rep to return to Salt Lake City. Unfortunately, senior management is not always so enlightened or effective. This presents an additional challenge for the sales manager.

The Hay Group, a consulting firm in Philadelphia, surveyed more than 750,000 middle managers in 1,000 corporations. The results indicate that between 1987 and 1990, the managers' most common estimation of their bosses' (CEOs or other senior managers) overall ability dropped from "generally high" to "frankly awful." This is cause for concern, as managers convey to their employees, either in words or in attitude, their own feelings about senior management.

As a sales manager, if you have concerns over the ability of senior management, you must try as much as possible to keep those feelings to yourself. If your boss is giving you a hard time, you must not take it out on your employees. It's important to shield your sales force from any barbs directed at you or them by top management. Fear and loathing are contagious; any negative signals you send as a result of being pressured by top management will occupy your salespeople's thoughts and hinder their day-to-day performance.

It's not enough to shield your employees from barbs directed at you by your manager. You must actively defend them against unfair or unproductive decisions of top management.

At some point in your career, you may be pressured by senior management to take actions you know are not in the best interest of your reps or the company as a whole. It is your responsibility to do what you believe is right. Sometimes that means taking an unpopular stand.

I was asked by my manager, the vice president of sales, to be prepared to let go of Jeff, one of my sales reps, as part of a companywide layoff. Jeff had been a consistent contributor for the previous four years, but he'd had back-to-back quarters during which he had performed below quota.

I realized that most of Jeff's revenues were dependent on the Southern California aerospace industry, which was in a downturn and was largely responsible for his poor performance. At the same time, I knew there was a great deal of diversity in this market area. Although it was still in the midst of a recession, I thought the market would rebound in time.

I did some research, including talking to several Southern California headhunters about employment patterns in the area. The message I got was mixed. It would be difficult for me to defend my position on logic alone.

Finally, I gave up on all my research and recommended we keep Jeff anyway. I relied on a simple philosophical saying that goes something like this: "When you are clear about what to do next, take action. When you aren't, pause."

This was one of the most difficult stands I have ever had to take in my sales management career. It's not the most politically correct thing to counter your boss right before the announcement of a layoff. You could be gone too.

Over the course of several weeks, the vice president of sales listened to my many arguments in favor of keeping this rep despite my doubts about the Southern California market. In the end, he relented and Jeff stayed. At present, the economy has picked up in Southern California, new accounts have opened, former accounts have expanded their budgets, and Jeff has increased his sales revenues more than fourfold during the past six months.

At some point in your career, you will inevitably be tested in ways similar to those described above. How you handle these interactions will strongly influence the productivity and loyalty of your sales team. Whether or not you defend your own positions and support your salespeople in front of senior management, word will get around. You will be viewed either as someone to follow or someone to work around.

If you are a "yes man" (or woman), your sales teams will have little respect for you. But if you stand up for your employees and challenge unfair or unproductive decisions in a tactful and diplomatic way, even if you don't win, you'll be viewed as a leader.

If you challenge the way things are done, your salespeople will follow your lead. Can you imagine the impact of having a large number of people change their own way into a better way?

Unfortunately, many sales managers are reluctant to take a stand that might be unpopular with senior management, for fear of losing their jobs. As a result, their sales reps become more distrustful ("even the boss won't stand up for us"), and productivity suffers.

This fear is largely unjustified. Over the years I've taken many stands against the safe and secure political route, in the interests of my employees. Surprisingly, everything seemed to work out, for the employees and for me. I was never reprimanded, demoted, or fired as a result.

If you strongly believe in a position that is the opposite of your manager's and if you have a compelling reason for your stance, the reasonable manager will respect you for it. If you are working in a company with unreasonable management, it may be time for you to reconsider your own career options.

Open Communications

Every once in a while, I ask my salespeople what my boss and I are doing wrong and what we're doing right. When I asked this question to a group of salespeople, they told me that one thing we're doing right is communicating with them. They like the rumor control voice mail messages from my manager and the fireside chats I have with them, in which I probe their feelings about how things are going in the company and in their jobs.

Open communications are essential to maintaining a high energy, productive, high morale environment. Sales reps may be hundreds or thousands of miles from headquarters. It's easy for them to feel abandoned or out of touch with what's going on in the rest of the company. It's important to keep the lines of communication open.

Communication is especially important in an era of downsizing, when rumors can run rampant. Employees will naturally (usually secretly) start looking elsewhere for work if they hear rumors that suggest their jobs are in jeopardy. Whether or not their fears are warranted, how you as a sales manager handle this situation will determine whether they remain loyal to the company or bolt at the first opportunity.

Tom, a rep whose performance was deteriorating, began to ask me frequently about the future of our company. Tom's uncle, a pension fund manager, had been giving him negative information about the company, information that was common knowledge in financial circles but was news to me.

I told Tom the truth, that I hadn't heard anything to indicate the company's future was in jeopardy. We'd gone through some directional changes under a new CEO, but it seemed to me the company was now on the right course.

I could tell that Tom distrusted the company line on future takeovers (the company said there was no possibility of a takeover), so I expected that in time he would leave. Instead, he pursued another option, which I discovered by accident.

When I called Tom's home one evening, I was connected to his answering machine. The recorded greeting in Tom's voice caught me off guard. The message was: "Thanks for calling Horizon Freight Auditing Company. If you would like to leave a message, do so at the beep." With great reluctance and anger, I left a message questioning whether I had the right household.

The next day, I could have grilled Tom about the recorded message and questioned whether his poor performance was a result of his moonlighting. My better judgment told me to keep quiet. I ignored the message and made no future comments about it. I understood why Tom had started an outside venture; he was the most fearful of all of my staff about being laid off.

Tom realized I had caught him in the act, and he tried to explain the recorded message by saying the freight auditing business was his wife's. I didn't argue with him, and I didn't pursue the issue. Instead, I concentrated on working with him to improve his sales numbers.

Tom clearly appreciated the fact that I dropped the issue of his moonlighting. As a result of my treating him with respect and trust, his performance improved significantly. He became one of the top five salespeople in the district, building his territory from $200,000 in annual sales to $2 million over four years—a growth rate far exceeding that of the overall market.

Communication is especially crucial to retaining top salespeople in turbulent times. Successful salespeople have a high level of autonomy and only a moderate degree of affiliation to others in the company. If they sense that the company is in trouble or their jobs are in jeopardy, they may start looking elsewhere unless you take steps to prevent it. High achievers want to work for companies that offer plenty of opportunity for the future. They want to be part of a winning team. If they see that a company is not growing, there's no reason to stay.

This doesn't mean that all successful salespeople will jump ship as soon as it begins to sink. This will occur primarily in those companies that have gone through repeated layoffs without tying the layoff to a specific purpose, or communicating the truth to employees.

You cannot be responsible for what senior management tells employees, but you are responsible for your own communications. If you are honest and open with your sales reps, they are more likely to stay with the firm, even in troubled times.

The Humane Approach to Layoffs

The constant threat of being laid off will inevitably drive some employees to look for other job options. As a sales manager, you must be sensitive to these concerns.

If the threat of a layoff is real, you must openly communicate what you know about the layoff to your staff and help them prepare for it in advance. This approach will minimize disruption and prevent rumors from spreading and further depressing morale.

If your division or company is about to be acquired, let your reps know, as much as you can, what to expect from the new company. Is it likely to lay off workers? What will the new work environment be like?

Warning employees ahead of time that a layoff is possible makes them feel more in control of the situation. It gives them time to decide whether they are happy with the company's future direction and time to find a different job if they are not, or if they feel certain their jobs will be eliminated.

Treating layoffs humanely will benefit you, your salespeople, and your company. The laid-off salesperson will feel respected by your company and will work to ensure an orderly transition of responsibility, which will be reassuring to customers. And those left after the layoffs will have more respect for a boss who has handled the downsizing humanely.

The Financial Side of Sales Management

In the early 1980s, Jane Mouton and Robert Blake developed a management model that stresses the need for managers to be task-oriented and people-oriented. According to Mouton and Blake, having a low orientation in either area will reduce managerial effectiveness.[2]

The Mouton and Blake model can be modified in the 1990s to add a third dimension: finance. Today, the successful sales manager must be financially accountable as well as task- and people-oriented. The sales manager today must adopt a new, profit-oriented mindset. This is a challenge for managers and salespeople alike, who were accustomed in the past to being rewarded for doing "whatever it takes to get the order."

The four corners of the grid in Figure 2-1 represent four distinct management styles.

A. *Mushroom Manager*. This manager's philosophy is "keep them in the dark." Salespeople are never sure of this manager's expectations. Salespeople are given no guidance on how to achieve sales goals and no information about the company's financial performance. This type of manager makes no attempt to develop rapport with employees or otherwise show concern for them.

B. *Attila the Hun*. This authoritarian task master requires

Figure 2-1. Management style grid.

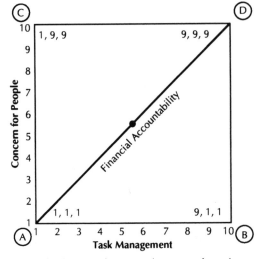

Note: The three numbers in each corner refer to the horizontal, vertical, and diagonal axes, respectively.

extensive paperwork and a high level of activity from salespeople. He or she does not communicate financial information to employees, except to use it as a threat against them. This type does little to build a social climate.

C. *Great Communicator.* This manager constantly looks for ways to build a better social environment for salespeople and keeps them well informed about the company's finances, but is weak in task management.

D. *Renaissance Manager.* This is the ideal model, the manager who excels at task management, has a strong concern for people, freely (and frequently) communicates information about the company's financial picture, and ties performance reviews to company results. The Renaissance Manager makes salespeople feel they are trusted to set their own goals and structure their own activities.

The Move to Strategic Selling

The financially oriented sales manager must ensure that salespeople pursue only profitable sales opportunities. During the 1980s, salespeople were encouraged to go after any and every sale, using whatever resources they needed from the company in order to close the sale. Today, the sales rep is expected to approach each sales situation from a profit perspective.

The physical and human resources of the corporation are dwindling. Sales managers and reps are now expected to do more with less. The company can no longer afford to chase marginally profitable projects that it might have pursued in the past. The salesperson must spend time only on those efforts that are going to generate the greatest return for the company.

Early in my career, when I was a salesman for a specialty chemicals company, I pursued a project to prevent scale deposition in evaporators that make refined sugar.

The evaporators had two sides, separated by stainless steel. On one side was the process flow or the sugar. On the other side was water at high temperatures, which helped to evaporate the process sugar to achieve a higher sugar concentration. The scaling problems were occurring on the sugar side of the evaporator.

Although my company had the expertise to control scale deposition on the water side of the evaporators, we didn't have a product that could go into the sugar side. I saw an opportunity for us to learn how to prevent deposition on this side as well.

On presenting my idea to headquarters, I received a "go get 'em" response. I met with our customer's process engineers and for a few months my company examined the technical feasibility of this new application. Although it never did turn into a product, I was impressed with this first experience of introducing a new product application and having my company take it seriously. I had many more of these experiences during my early career, and they were terrific motivators for me.

Salespeople need to feel they're a vital part of the company. When they see their recommendations taken seriously, they are driven to be even more productive. I've seen salespeople operate on pure adrenaline when they feel their work is important to the company's future.

Today, because of downsizing and the increased pressure for short-term profits, any new idea from the field must pass a much more stringent qualification process than in the past. The payback time and return on investment of any potential application must reach certain levels if the idea is to be pursued.

Here are the four questions to ask before you pass on your salespeople's product/project ideas to corporate headquarters:

1. Does this idea apply to a key market segment of my sales district?
2. Will the idea apply to other districts in the country?
3. Can we implement this idea with minor modifications to an existing product?
4. Is there acceptance of this new idea from innovators within the targeted market segment?

If you answered yes to all four questions, there is a high probability that this idea is worth pursuing. If not, you may want to reconsider.

In general, it's best to pursue those ideas that align closely with your existing products first, since these are likely to require the least time and effort to implement. It's also wise not to pursue too many ideas simultaneously. Better to penetrate one market extremely well than target half a dozen ineffectively.

Profitable vs. Unprofitable Selling

To sell profitably, sales managers must start looking at more than the typical expenses like salary, travel, lodging, and other typical expense areas. They must also take into account the cost of time spent on sales calls.

A common estimate of selling time per hour is $250 for a single face-to-face sales call. Because the cost of a sales call is so high, the sales manager must make sure that reps are spending their time profitably.

To show the difference between profitable and unprofitable selling, let's focus on two salespeople, Jack and Susan. Jack and Susan each have $50,000 in sales in a one-month period (Figure 2-2). But Susan's superior qualifying skills results in her generating $50,000 in revenues from only 10 sales calls. It takes Jack three times as many calls to generate the same amount of revenue. Susan's sales calls expenses are $2,500 for the month; Jack's are $7,500.

Assuming that both reps' travel, meals, and other expenses are similar, Susan has generated three times as much profit as

Figure 2-2. Profitable vs. unprofitable selling.

	Jack	Susan
Sales revenue	$50,000	$50,000
Number of sales calls	30	10
Total sales call cost ($250/call)	$ 7,500	$ 2,500
Sales call cost as percentage of sales	15%	5%

Jack. Although this month their revenue performance may be equal, in the long term Jack's performance will start to suffer unless he learns how to work smart, not just hard.

The new, profit-conscious sales environment goes counter to the "killer instincts" of salespeople to "get the order, no matter what." Salespeople want to win every sales situation they encounter. Forcing them to consider the profit implications before they go after a sale is like placing a leash on a pit bull. Salespeople are used to thinking in terms of revenues, not profits. It's up to the sales manager to educate reps about the bigger financial picture of the business, not just the revenue side, so that they'll understand why they are free to pursue certain sales opportunities and not others.

Otherwise, when their unprofitable ideas are rejected one after another, they may wrongly conclude that the company doesn't care. If they have detailed information about the company's finances and how their actions affect the bottom line, they will be more likely to accept or at least tolerate the leash.

Opening the Company Books

In the profit-conscious nineties, every employee in the company must understand the impact of their actions on the financial health of the business. This lesson was driven home to me a couple of years ago when I invited Randy, the manufacturing manager of our company, to attend one of our sales meetings and speak to us about how our financial forecasts affected his department.

After hearing what Randy had to say, my staff and I developed an instant appreciation for the impact of our actions on the financial health of the company. He showed us that, as a result of our forecasting inaccuracies, our company had accrued inventory overcharges in excess of $1.4 million during the previous year.

This news was staggering to me, and it made me more keenly aware of the sales department's need for access to frequent and detailed information about the company's financial status.

In his popular book, *The Great Game of Business*, Jack Stack discussed the transformation of his company, Springfield Manufacturing, after the company's books were opened to all employees. Since many of the employees had never seen financial statements before, they had to learn how to read and understand them. But after a bit of education, they could easily look at the financials and understand the impact, positive or negative, of their actions on the company's profitability. As a result of giving this detailed information to employees, Stack writes, over a three-year period (1983–1986) sales grew more than 30 percent, whereas Springfield went from a loss of $60,488 in their first year to a pretax earnings of $2.7 million without a single layoff.[3] Sales managers should do this as well. Unless the sales manager has the company books open on a regular basis, salespeople will not be able to connect their own actions to the financial health of the company. If senior management does not volunteer to share detailed financial information with the sales department, you must ask for it and keep asking until you get it. It may require asking senior management. In my experience, they are willing to do this when they understand what it means.

It's not enough to be given quarterly reports. The sales manager needs to keep the sales force abreast of changes in the company's financial situation at least on a monthly basis.

A good place to start is to look at a breakdown of the company's average dollar of revenue, with a pretax profit goal in mind (Figure 2-3).

Figure 2-3 shows that for every $1.00 of revenue, 24 cents goes to selling expenses. Pretax profit is just 2 percent, so if commission expenses or any other selling expense exceeds 3 percent, the company will have no pretax profit.

Once salespeople see the "big picture" of the company's financial situation, they will be better able to understand how the sales department's expenses affect corporate profitability. With

Figure 2-3. Average dollar of revenue.

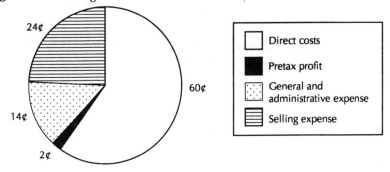

this big picture in mind, you can review with your reps their monthly expenses (Figure 2-4) and focus on how to correct any negative variances that will ultimately have an impact on corporate profits.

Giving salespeople this detailed information about how their actions affect corporate profitability is the best way to eliminate the attitude of "anything it takes to get the order."

For a long time, Frank, one of my sales reps, used to give away supplies to customers and prospects. One day, I reviewed my supply budget and discovered this rep was responsible for 80 percent of the total expenses for the region.

I called Frank into my office and explained to him in detail how our expense budget was determined, the amount that was in it, and how big a piece of the budget he was responsible for using up. "When you give away items that cost $300 or $400," I told him, "it makes us go over budget and affects the profitability of our region." Until this conversation, Frank had had no idea of the impact of his giving away supplies.

It takes a while for salespeople to get used to the idea of being accountable for sticking to budget limits. At first, Frank was defensive when I questioned him about giving away supplies. "It's tough out there," he protested. "I need to do this to get the order. . . ." With the monthly selling expense roll-up in front of him, however, it was easier for him to accept the idea that he had to change his behavior.

Frank is still winning the same number of orders, but without giving away supplies. Give people a crutch and they'll come to believe they can't walk without it—until you take it away.

Figure 2-4. Breakdown of sales department expenses.

	April		
	Actual	Plan	Variance
Orders	75,000	100,000	− 25
Salary	$4,000	$4,000	0
Commission	2,250	4,000	1,750
Fringe benefits	1,000	1,000	0
Travel	1,200	1,200	0
E/M/L	592	600	8
Telephone	400	450	50
Leased auto	500	500	0
Total costs	$9,942	$11,750	1,808
Exp. as a percentage of orders	13.0%	10.5%	

Monitoring the Changing Financial Picture. Salespeople need to have a good idea of how each market segment is performing over time. This can be shown by means of a simple pie chart (Figure 2-5) that indicates corporate revenues by market segment. By monitoring these figures over time in your monthly sales meetings, you will be able to pinpoint possible trouble, identify trends, and correct problems before they become overwhelming.

For example, suppose that sales to the chemical industry drop unexpectedly, from 25 percent to 20 percent, over a one-month period. Could it be due to economic forces, or is the competition taking 5 percent market share from the chemical industry? The salespeople, working with the sales manager, can explore the cause of the problem.

If the answer is that competitive forces are causing the decline, the sales manager's role becomes one of a detective. The manager directs the sales force to spend their selling efforts over the next quarter visiting chemical industry accounts. The purpose of the visits is to find out which accounts have purchased competitors' products and the reasons why, before additional market share losses occur.

You can also compare the twelve-month pipeline for each

Figure 2-5. Sales revenue by market segment.

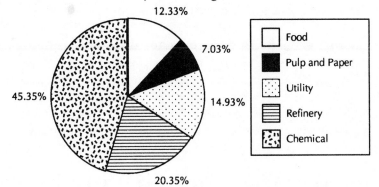

sales rep with historical sales figures, by market segment, to spot emerging trends. Suppose that 20 percent of the accounts in a rep's twelve-month pipeline are from the university segment, which historically accounts for only 10 percent of sales. This signals a major increase in university business. To take advantage of it, you can instruct your salespeople to concentrate even more of their time on university accounts over the next six to twelve months.

Developing an Effective Compensation Plan

The sale's manager's financial responsibility includes the development of a compensation plan that is profitable for the company as well as motivating and financially rewarding for salespeople. Many salespeople feel that the more they sell, the more money they make for the company. The truth is, some commission plans are set up poorly, resulting in salespeople making a lucrative compensation package even as the company's profitability keeps dropping.

Let's say a product lists for $50,000. By being willing to sell it for $40,000, a salesperson may be able to sell ten units. If the rep sells the product for $45,000, he or she may be able to sell eight units. A commission plan that pays on volume would reward the rep for discounting 20 percent, because revenues at that discount level would be $400,000 (10 times $40,000) rather than $360,000 (8 times $45,000).

If it cost $30,000 to manufacture the product, ten sales at $45,000 each would generate $100,000 gross profits, whereas the eight sales at $45,000 each will generate $120,000 gross profits. The salesperson is making more money on $400,000 volume, but the company is losing $20,000 in gross profits.

Many companies, rather than continuing to give high payouts for average or poor performance, are restructuring commission plans so that only salespeople who bring in profitable business are given significant rewards, rather than giving equal commissions.

Determining Average Compensation. The first step in developing a compensation plan is to determine what you want your total average compensation (salary plus commission plus bonus, if any) to be relative to other companies in your industry. Do you want to be in the top ten percentile or the top 50 percentile?

Suppose you decide on an average compensation figure of $60,000, divided equally between salary and commission. You can calculate at quota that a salesperson will be able to make $30,000 in commissions. If the average quota is $1 million, the average commission rate is 3 percent.

The plan must be structured so that a blowout year in commissions will not lead to reduced profitability. Before implementing any plan, I recommend that you hire a reputable compensation consultant. With his or her assistance, you will be able to set up models to look at the potential financial effects of a proposed plan versus your current plan. The net result will be a fair and profitable plan for the company and the salespeople.

Whatever plan you choose, make sure that it's simple, so that salespeople know exactly how much they will earn in commissions on a given sale. Otherwise, it will not be as effective a motivational tool.

Types of Compensation Plans. There are four basic compensation plans for salespeople. They include:

1. Straight salary
2. Straight commission
3. Salary plus commission or bonus
4. Salary plus commission and bonus

To motivate selling behavior positively, selection of the right commission structure is crucial. For instance, a straight salary structure should be selected only if one or more of these conditions exist:

- Sales are largely influenced by factors outside of salesperson's control (e.g., a start-up company introducing new products).
- Sales cycles are long (1.5 years or longer).
- Repeat business from existing customers is more important than finding new accounts.

A straight commission structure will be most motivating in those environments where the skills, knowledge, and behavior of the salesperson are the sole determining factors in getting the order.

As you can see from these two extremes, it's important to match the appropriate commission structure to a specific selling environment. Selection of the right commission structure will reduce turnover and increase sales growth. The wrong structure will result in unhappy employees, a high rate of turnover, and depressed sales.

Most companies consider a middle-of-the-road plan, such as salary plus commission or bonus. This is the best approach when most sales situations involve teamwork with inside support people, repeat business is an important factor, and salespeople must also develop new accounts on a regular basis.

By setting up a commission plan with two categories, one for low margin sales and the other for high margin sales, a company can motivate salespeople to sell more high margin products and minimize discounting of the products.

For example, a company might divide its products into two categories, according to their gross profit margins (GPM), as shown in Figure 2-6.

Suppose a salesperson is at 80% of quota for the quarter, and he sells a $50,000 Level One product, or discounts a Level Two product to bring the gross profit margin below 45%. In either case, he will receive a 3% commission, or $1,500. If the rep sells a Level Two product without discounting below 45%, his commission on the sale would be double—6 percent, or $3,000.

Figure 2-6. Two-tier commission structure.

	Commission Structure	
	Level One Products	*Level Two Products*
Quarterly Quota	*0–45% GPM*	*> 45% GPM*
0–75%	1%	3%
76–100%	3%	6%
>100%	4%	8%

Your compensation plan should tie in to corporate goals. These could be anything from penetrating new markets to increasing sales from new products.

Many companies are looking at ways to increase gross profit margins. The two-tiered commission structure outlined in Figure 2-6 addresses this goal. There also may be secondary goals, such as increasing sales from new products. The best way to meet that goal would be by means of a salary plus commission plus bonus structure. For example, set a product mix goal for selling new products as 25 percent of the total product mix for a given quarter and reward those who reach this product mix with a $1,000 bonus. The two-tiered commission plan outlined above, with this added bonus for selling new products, will address both the primary and secondary goals of the marketing department.

Implementing the Plan. Many salespeople welcome the new-found corporate focus on bottom-line profits. They see it as a much needed change, an antidote to the "anything goes" mentality of the 1970s and 1980s that helped lead to the downsizing and takeovers.

It's easy to be philosophical when your earning potential is not being affected. The question is: How will average and poor performers react to decreased commissions when salespeople become the next targets?

The answer to that question is being played out in sales departments throughout the country. Reduced commissions will be a fact of life in many corporations in the coming decade, as companies restructure their commission plans to reward salespeople for the quality (i.e., profitability) of their efforts, not just the quantity.

How the sales manager handles the restructuring of the commission plan will determine how salespeople will react. If the manager imposes a new commission plan and tells reps they can "take it or leave it," the top salespeople are likely to leave. But if he or she explains why the commission budget has been changed and shows clearly how it is tied to corporate profitability, they are more likely to understand and accept it.

Loyalty in an Era of Uncertainty

A survey conducted by *Industry Week* asked respondents to rank six suggested factors that foster employee loyalty.[4] The respondents ranked them in the following order of importance: (1) recognition, (2) challenging work, (3) increased pay, (4) promotions, (5) dynamic boss, and (6) years of service. Unfortunately, most of these factors are no longer available as tools for the sales manager to use in winning the loyalty of the sales force. In this new era of job insecurity, the sales manager must use a different approach.

Expanding the Concept of Career Path

In the past, sales managers could offer their top performers a promotion, a fancy new title, and a hefty pay increase. Today, there are fewer positions available, and there is limited money for raises.

With fewer opportunities to promote and recognize sales reps, the sales manager must now find more creative ways to help them develop their careers and thus keep their loyalty. That includes expanding the concept of career paths to include lateral moves within the firm, or to new jobs in other companies.

The sales manager will have to become a career counselor, working with employees to determine their strengths and weaknesses and what types of career moves seem most appropriate. This will require a seasoned manager who understands the functional skills necessary for different positions, within or outside of the company.

In the 1990s, the human resources department may not have the time or resources to manage the training function in your company. Today, the sales manager must become actively involved in training, learning about employees' needs and interests, and recommending appropriate training programs.

It's a good idea to sit down with your salespeople individually every six to twelve months and review their career goals. Then, see to it that they get the training they need to qualify for their next career move. Do you have a salesperson with strong potential for a sales management career? Send her to a solid coaching or other management development program. Has one of your reps expressed an interest in a technical support position? Enroll him in a technical training course.

When sales managers show a genuine interest in the career development of their employees, the employees will respond with a strengthened commitment to the company. And ironically, providing workers with training that will make them more marketable to other firms will increase the probability that they will stay where they are.

Unfortunately, many companies are reluctant to train workers in the skills they need to advance their careers for fear they will leave the company. The company's view is "why spend hundreds of thousands of dollars on training if the employees are just going to be more marketable?" This creates a self-fulfilling prophecy. Companies don't invest in training, and the employees leave anyway—starting with the best performers.

Periodically ask your salespeople, "What is the one thing that I or the company can do to help you advance professionally?" Don't assume you know the answer. One sales manager of a beverage company asked this question of his veteran salespeople. To his surprise, they said they wanted more sales training. Upper management, although skeptical of the value of additional training, invested $20,000 in a two-day training program, which was enthusiastically received by the salespeople.

Smart companies provide training, even with the knowledge that employees may leave eventually. Companies such as Apple Computer are now offering their own in-house management programs that focus on skills that will make their employees marketable to other companies. This embodies the implicit contract between employer and employee in the 1990s: "We'll prepare you, in the event we can no longer keep you, but we ask for your loyalty as long as you stay."

The Need for a Company Vision

But people development is only one side of the loyalty equation. For companies to win the loyalty of their salespeople, they must also have a compelling vision.

As Figure 2-7 suggests, even without a company vision, there is still the possibility of loyalty to the sales manager. But personal allegiance will only go so far. In the absence of a compelling vision, top salespeople will leave the company as soon as they find a better opportunity, even if they feel loyal to their manager.

Only those companies that have a compelling vision for the future will win their employees' loyalty. Communicating that corporate vision is one of the CEO's most important functions.

The sales manager cannot control the CEO. But he or she has the responsibility to stress to senior management the importance of developing and communicating a strong vision of where the company is headed, in terms of products, customers, and markets. Salespeople need to know their company has a future and that they will have a significant role in it.

Only if salespeople feel they are genuinely important to their companies will they give their loyalty to them. The best way to make them feel they are important is to involve them in the strategic direction of the company. Ask for their input about new products, new markets, and new strategies. Lobby senior management to include salespeople in the strategic planning process.

Figure 2-7. Employee loyalty model.

The choices for American companies are simple: either instill a sense of vision and belonging to the company's future or face the fact that you are going to lose your best salespeople and managers. If they sense that the company's future or their role in it is unclear, the top salespeople will take their loyalty elsewhere.

Notes

1. George Lumsden, *Building a Winning Sales Force* (Chicago: Dartnell Corp., 1986), 11. Reprinted with the permission of the Dartnell Corporation, Chicago, Illinois.
2. Robert R. Blake and Jane S. Mouton, *The New Managerial Grid* (Houston: Gulf Publishing, 1978).
3. Jack Stack, *The Great Game of Business* (New York: Doubleday, 1992), 3.
4. Joseph F. McKenna, "What Can Restore Fading Loyalty?" *Industry Week*, February 4, 1991: 50.

Chapter 3

Self-Management In the Sales Organization

Self-Management: The Wave of the Future

Self-management is an idea whose time has come. The typical sales manager in the 1990s has more direct reports and less time to provide day-to-day direction to them. Salespeople today must operate with far more independence than in the past. They must make strategy decisions that formerly would have been made by the sales manager, must assume some of the functions previously carried out by the marketing department, and must take more responsibility than ever before for setting goals and achieving results. To carry out their new and expanded roles successfully, they must learn how to manage themselves.

Empowerment: The Foundation of Self-Management

In a previous sales management position, I was approached by Chuck, one of my salespeople, who asked if he could leave his demo unit at a potential customer's site for a few days. I was surprised by the question, since I am used to my reps taking responsibility for their actions.

How could I answer Chuck's question, when only he had the information to make the decision about the demo unit? Only he knew what objectives he wanted to accomplish by leaving the unit at the site, what his demo schedule looked like over the course of the next week, and so on. I told Chuck that what he did with the demo unit was strictly up to him.

Chuck was part of a new division I'd inherited. He had been accustomed to a completely different management environment. Until now, Chuck had always been told what to do and when and how to do it. He was never asked for his opinion or given responsibility for making adult decisions and carrying them out.

Now that Chuck was asked to make his own decisions, he felt paralyzed. As a result, he was initially one of the company's worst performing sales reps.

The biggest roadblock to Chuck's performance was his own inability to take charge—until one day I sat down with him and told him that his success would depend on taking the initiative and not looking over his shoulder for constant approval from me. I repeated this message frequently to Chuck, and eventually his confidence soared and his sales numbers followed.

When managers treat their employees like children, when they require them to ask permission for every action they take or decision they make, the employees never learn how to manage themselves and their time. Managers no longer have the time to closely monitor their employees. Only by empowering salespeople to take responsibility for themselves will they develop the skills and maturity needed to become self-managing.

Jerry is another example of how empowering salespeople can produce tremendous results. Jerry had been complaining that the marketing department was not holding enough seminars in his territory and others. As a result, they were not generating the new leads that were desperately needed.

Jerry and I discussed the need for him to take charge rather than sit back and wait for others to do the job for him. I suggested that Jerry start planning and organizing the seminars himself, and I gave him the opportunity to chair a part of our sales meeting (which my boss attended) and announce that he would now be in charge of developing a seminar series in our region. His message was well received by the other salespeople and by my manager.

Once Jerry quit complaining and started taking charge, the results were astounding. He formed a self-directed team of salespeople to conduct the seminars. He asked each one of his peers to select the type of seminars they felt were most valuable. Each was asked to chair one of them.

Chairing a seminar is no small task. The chairperson's responsibility is to become the expert on the seminar topic and to arrange for other people and equipment resources from headquarters to be at the seminars. In addition to organizing and planning, the designated chairperson leads the seminar in his or her own territory as well as five other sales territories.

Throughout Jerry's seminar project, I praised him for his tremendous initiative in developing a self-directed team to orchestrate the seminars. Jerry welcomed my support in this huge coordination effort, as he still was expected to exceed his sales goals. The end result was a highly charged salesperson who makes things happen.

Empowerment is an exciting prospect for many independent-minded employees, but it can be scary for those who are accustomed to implementing the decisions of others rather than making and carrying out their own. And it can be unsettling to those who are used to blaming others for their own shortcomings.

It takes time for most employees to feel comfortable with empowerment. However, once they get used to the idea of taking responsibility for themselves, in my experience they become more mature, more productive, and far more satisfied with themselves and their jobs.

Empowerment is the foundation of self-management. By empowering your salespeople to make their own decisions and allowing them to participate in the decisions you make, you are setting the stage for a Progressive Goal Management system, a powerful self-management tool.

The Progressive Goal Management (PGM) System

Progressive Goal Management (PGM) is a goal-setting system that tries to improve individual and company performance by teaching salespeople how to become effective self-managers. "Progressive" implies the development of successive goals from one (quarterly) goal period to the next, leading to a specific outcome at the end of the year, such as "increasing the number of new customers by fifteen." These individual goals contribute to the achievement of specific corporate goals, such as "increasing pre-tax profits to 15–20 percent."

The PGM system balances salespeople's desire for independence and control with their need for feedback and guidance. Under the system, sales reps set their own goals and rate themselves on their success in achieving them (discussed in a later section). This makes them feel more responsible for, and in control of, their success. At the same time, the manager gives them frequent feedback to make sure that they stay on the path that will lead to achievement. Instead of the manager acting as a dictator or controller, he or she serves as a consultant and coach.

The accomplishment of goals under the PGM system is the basis for the salesperson's year-end performance rating. Because salespeople have set their own goals and receive feedback throughout the year on how they are progressing toward achieving them, there are no surprises in year-end performance reviews.

Guidelines for Developing a PGM System

Before we get into the specifics of building a Progressive Goal Management system, let's look at the three major ingredients required for such a system to produce optimum results.

1. *Goals must be written at least quarterly.* One Fortune 500 company I'm familiar with gives its employees the authority to develop their own business goals. When I asked a sales rep from this company how he had fared on the five business goals he'd developed, he told me he didn't meet even one of them. The reason, it soon became clear, was that goals were developed only once a year. If goals had been written on a quarterly basis, the salesperson would have been better able to assess his progress, and his manager would have been able to assist the rep in reaching these goals before year end.

It's difficult to stay focused on a single set of goals for an entire year, without losing interest or veering off track. For this reason, under the PGM system, salespeople track existing goals and write a new set of goals at least on a quarterly basis.

2. *Feedback from manager to salesperson must be given at least quarterly, and preferably monthly.* Once annual goals are set, many sales managers don't bother to give feedback to salespeople about how they are progressing toward achieving the goals. This can lead to major surprises at year-end reviews.

Frequent feedback is vital if salespeople are to achieve the goals they set. Under the PGM system, feedback is given regularly so that salespeople know where they stand, and so that sales managers can help poor performers get back on the right track before too much time has passed.

I give feedback to my salespeople on a monthly basis, circulating their lists of quarterly goals and letting them know whether or not their performance is leading them in the direction of achieving those goals. This monthly feedback allows me to spot problems and redirect the salesperson's goals, if needed, at the next quarterly goal-writing session.

3. *Goals must measurably improve performance.* The question to ask in formulating goals under the PGM system is "will this goal lead to improved performance?" If the answer is no, the goal is inadequate. For example, random activity such as doing a mailing to a list of customers is an inadequate goal unless it is done with the intent of generating a specific number of sales leads and with a specific revenue goal in mind.

Routine vs. Creative Goals

There are two levels of goals that employees set under the PGM system: Routine and Creative. Routine goals deal with such things as achieving sales quotas, keeping expenses at a certain percentage of budget, and adding prospects to the pipeline. Creative goals are intended to take the salesperson's territory to higher levels of performance than if nothing beyond the routine were done. An example of a Creative goal is developing a newsletter targeted to a group of potential customers in a certain industry.

Creative goals are strategic in nature. They are meant to stretch salespeople, to get them to move into new and unfamiliar territory that will yield greater productivity in the long run. They are intended to prevent salespeople from staying in a rut, developing the same goals quarter after quarter because it's comfortable to do so.

Whereas Creative goals are meant to stretch salespeople, they are not intended to be used as a weapon against them. For salespeople to be willing to take the risk of pursuing challenging Creative goals, they must know they will not be punished if they don't succeed in achieving them.

Realistic vs. Dream Range

In addition to goal levels, there are two ranges for PGM goal-setting: Realistic and Dream. Goals that fall into the Realistic range are those that, whether they are Routine or Creative, can reasonably be achieved by the average salesperson during a given period. Goals in the Dream range are those that represent exceptional performance. If closing three major sales during a given period is a Realistic goal, closing five might be a Dream goal.

Under the PGM system, salespeople are required to write down a Realistic and a Dream range for each goal they set. This forces them to think seriously about what is required to achieve a goal and helps them to develop over time a more realistic conception of what is or isn't possible to achieve.

There's nothing wrong in shooting for the Dream range, as one salesperson I interviewed reminded me. When I hired Robin, I asked him, "What's the one behavior you want me to avoid, that would demotivate you?" He replied, "When I say I am going to make an outrageous sales number, don't tell me it can't be done." The Dream range is a way for people like Robin to shoot for the stars without being shot down, since failure to achieve a Dream result is not considered negative under the PGM system, just as the failure to achieve an aggressive Creative goal is not.

Learning to Set Goals

When salespeople begin developing goals under the PGM system, they tend to focus on Routine rather than Creative goals that would stretch them. That's okay. It's difficult enough for salespeople to learn to write effective Routine goals. At the start, don't discourage them by asking for more Creative goals. However, if after a number of quarters they continue in the Routine mode, you may want gently to nudge them in the direction of developing their potential by means of Creative goals.

The eight questions that follow will guide your salespeople in developing goals:

1. What is the final result you want to achieve by the end of the year? This may be a certain sales figure, number of new customers, etc. All quarterly goals will be aimed at achieving this year-end result.
2. What are the obstacles toward achieving this result?
3. What goals would help you overcome these obstacles?
4. What are the strengths and weaknesses of your sales territory? What goals would capitalize on the strengths and/or minimize the weaknesses?
5. If you did nothing differently this quarter than you did the last, what impact would this have on your final result?
6. Of the goals that you have accomplished during the last quarter, which ones are progressive, i.e., which ones build on a previous goal? (An example might be a goal of selling ten units of a new product vs. a goal of selling seven units of the product during the previous quarter/ goal period.)
7. How did you achieve this progress?
8. Of the goals you failed to accomplish during the last quarter, what could you have done differently in order to meet them?

Trying to get salespeople to think about their territories in terms of such strategic questions is quite difficult. Salespeople are conditioned to react to the moment—to respond to quotas, leads, and phone calls from customers in a quick and decisive way. They are unaccustomed to thinking ahead, which is necessary to produce long-term productivity improvements. The PGM system helps them to look toward the future rather than focusing solely on the immediate situation.

Developing Creative Goals

To help the sales rep develop Creative goals, spend some time going over the above questions, focusing especially on those related to obstacles (2 and 3) and the one dealing with not doing anything differently (5). These questions will keep the rep focused on achieving long-term, more difficult goals.

In addition to guiding them through the questions, make sure to provide your salespeople with ample encouragement and support for pursuing Creative goals. Many salespeople suffer from inertia. It's easy to get into the rut of pursuing Routine goals and tough to do the stretching required of Creative goals. It helps to give salespeople an extra push by working with them to develop these more difficult goals. Salespeople are motivated more by managers who work alongside them than by those who simply make demands on them.

Offer rewards for accomplishing Creative goals. When I ask my salespeople what form of reward they prefer for achieving certain objectives, cash is always the number one answer. Tying cash bonuses to achievement of quarterly Creative goals will emphasize the importance of these goals and will motivate salespeople to keep producing them.

Most important, make sure that you are not in any way interfering with your sales reps' ability to achieve their goals. To ensure this, have your reps assess your performance as a manager periodically, in order to identify any behaviors, attitudes, or other aspects of your management style that may be inhibiting their performance. (The management assessment process is discussed later in this chapter.)

Red Flags in the Goal-Setting Process

When your salespeople begin to develop goals under the PGM system, you should watch for some predictable red flags, goals that show the reps do not yet understand the purpose and mechanics of the goal-setting process.

The most common red flags are goals that have nothing to do with the achievement of a specific result. For example, I cringe when a sales rep writes a goal that consists of doing a direct mailing to a customer or prospect list with no indication of the number of leads he or she hopes to obtain. Without an objective in mind, such random activity is a waste of time.

One salesperson who actually wrote this goal of doing a direct mailing was, at the time, experiencing a significant decline in sales revenues because of a relative decline in the percentage of high-end products he was selling. He should have been focusing on goals that would address this serious problem.

Another sales rep got even further off track. One of the goals included in his quarterly list involved coaching a service engineer in another department in time management techniques, to make him more responsive in managing customer calls.

Goals must not be confused with activities. Goals *may be* activities, but only if they are squarely focused on achieving a specific outcome.

Although you may wince when reading some of the inappropriate goals that novices to the PGM system develop, it's important that you respond constructively. If you respond harshly to your salespeople's initial attempts at goal-setting, in the future you can expect them to write down only what they think you want to hear. And you can be sure they will never learn how to develop their own goal-setting capabilities.

Goal Setting for Beginners

The following story is typical of the learning process for salespeople who are new to the Progressive Goal Management system.

A while ago I hired a salesperson, Tom, to work in a location 1,200 miles from our regional office. After he had completed his orientation and training, I asked Tom to write down his goals for the first ninety days on the job.

Being an ambitious salesperson with a high need for achievement, Tom drafted his goals in less than thirty minutes. He knew exactly what he wanted to accomplish during his first quarter on the job.

1. To be able to give presentations on all of the company's products without any assistance.
   Realistic: 90 days   *Dream:* 60 days

2. To contact all customers in my territory and ascertain the level of customer satisfaction.
   Realistic: 90 days   *Dream:* 60 days

3. To increase the sales pipeline from $500,000 to more than $1 million.
   Realistic: $1.0 million   *Dream:* $1.3 million

When I read the list, it seemed to me that all three of Tom's goals were unrealistic, but I didn't say anything. It's important for salespeople to learn from their own mistakes, especially in the initial stages of goal-setting. Furthermore, there is no way for the sales manager to be sure of a new rep's capabilities. It's all too easy for the manager to prejudge and actually discourage a rep from accomplishing big things. Maybe Tom's goals were unrealistic, but maybe not. I have learned that a "wait-and-see" approach is the most effective.

After seventy-five days had passed, during one of my field trips I asked Tom how he was progressing. He said he had not yet contacted all of our customers (Goal 2) because he hadn't realized there were so many of them. He also mentioned that he was having difficulty making unassisted product presentations (Goal 1). I didn't press him for the reason.

After further probing, I learned that Tom hadn't allocated enough time to contact the customers in his territory. Instead, he had been busy hand delivering brochures to interested prospects.

On my return to the regional office, I sent Tom a brief letter summarizing my understanding of his progress. It was necessary for me to document what we discussed during the visit, since salespeople tend to think you will forget the conversations held during field trips as soon as you board the plane for home.

I didn't send a copy of the letter to my boss. It's important that my salespeople trust me, that they recognize I don't write such letters to cover myself but simply to document their progress.

After Tom's initial ninety-day goal period was over, I observed that he had been unable to meet any of his three major goals. At this point I assumed the role of coach, asking Tom what were the obstacles to achieving the goals.

Tom said he had underestimated the complexity of our technology and product applications, and that's why he had been unable to achieve Goal 1. This was a reasonable explanation.

With regard to the second goal, Tom said he realized that the problem wasn't really too many customers to contact. The trouble was that the company had not provided all the demo equipment he needed for the territory. As a result, he had to make multiple calls to keep the prospect's interest until the equipment arrived. Because of these multiple calls, he didn't have sufficient time to contact the customer base, which meant he was also unable to fulfill Goal 3, increasing the pipeline.

When I hear of an obstacle that is outside of the salesperson's control, I take action to remove it as soon as possible. In this case, I made sure that Tom had the proper amount of demo equipment in his territory within two weeks of our conversation.

Tom sat down in December and wrote an assessment of his initial ninety-day performance. It read as follows:

1. Am I disappointed with my progress relative to my expectations? Yes.

2. Do I have reasonable expectations that at the end of this quarter I can be where I originally expected to be and fulfilling the company's expectations as well? Taking all factors into consideration? Yes.

Then he wrote a new set of Routine goals for the next ninety-day period.

1. Increase the sales pipeline by $400,000, from the current $600,000 level to $1 million. Assuming that the average sale = $20,000, I must generate twenty new leads to increase the pipeline by $400,000. Assuming that one of eight contacts results in pipeline placement, I must make 160 contacts.
   Realistic: $1.0 million   *Dream:* $1.5 million

2. Send a letter of introduction by X to all current customers:
   Realistic: February   *Dream:* January

3. Be prepared to demo the Viking [equipment] to sales manager and applications manager by X:
   Realistic: February   *Dream:* January

This is a well-done, more realistic goal list. Note how this time around Tom lays out the details of how he will increase the pipeline. By thinking through the details of what is required to achieve a certain level of sales activity, he is less likely to become caught up in activity traps such as handing out brochures.

Overcoming Obstacles to Success

One strength of the Progressive Goal Management system is that it helps salespeople to identify and overcome obstacles to success that are unique to their territories. Ben's story is a good example.

Ben had more than twenty years of selling experience in the capital equipment industry when he joined my company and was assigned to my region. When he arrived on the scene, his territory's product mix was heavily skewed in favor of our lower priced products. This was in large part because the previous sales rep had felt uncomfortable presenting our higher priced products to customers, which involved working with PhD scientists. As a result, our presence at the major research organizations in the territory—a major potential source of high-end business—was poor.

To address this obstacle and improve the profitability of the territory, Ben developed the following goals:

1. Achieve a win/loss ratio in the low-end product area of:
   Realistic: 15 percent   *Dream:* 25 percent
2. Increase sales of high-end products, from the current 10 percent of total sales to:
   Realistic: 30 percent   *Dream:* 65 percent
3. Develop field demos for government accounts, to increase the number of new government orders from seven in the previous quarter to at least ten.
   Realistic: 10 orders   *Dream:* 12 orders
4. Develop field demos for potential college accounts, to increase the number of new college orders from fourteen to twenty.
   Realistic: 20 orders   *Dream:* 22 orders

Goals 1 and 2 are Routine, in that it's mandatory for Ben's long-term success to meet these goals. The last two are Creative; they go beyond the Routine with the aim of achieving longer term improvements.

Taking this proactive direction, Ben increased sales revenues in his territory over 50 percent within six months and is position-ing his territory for long-term growth.

The Importance of Being Supportive

The sales manager plays a vital role in helping salespeople learn how to develop their self-management skills with the help of the PGM system. An example from my own experience shows how this works.

Steve, who has been in sales for only two years, is one of my top-performing salespeople. When he first started setting goals, he stuck to Routine goals such as hitting his quota and keeping a sufficient number of prospects in the pipeline. Gradually, as I encouraged him to become more entrepreneurial, he started to achieve Creative goals that none of his more experienced prede-cessors had accomplished.

One of Steve's major industry segments was a small fish in the big pond of our company. Headquarters didn't have time to address the future needs of this market segment, so Steve decided to do so himself. He identified a need for a piece of equipment that would help a certain customer use our own products more effectively, then worked with an outside contractor to see that the equipment was built.

This achievement started out as a goal that Steve developed in the context of our Progressive Goal Management system. Steve initially wrote a goal of developing an automated system that would enable customers to use our products more effectively and thus maintain zero attrition in this customer segment. I recog-nized the importance of this goal and guided Steve through the process of acting as a project coordinator between our marketing department and the outside contractor. He did a wonderful job of communicating with the appropriate people inside and outside of our company.

As a result of this success, Steve's entrepreneurial flair has expanded into other areas, since he understands I will never criticize or doubt him. Instead, I empower him to make the decisions that will improve his performance and strengthen his confidence.

Steve formed a local partnership with another manufacturer, whereby our two companies' products are combined to enhance the efficiency of a key customer segment. This innovative idea will result in new leads that will eventually turn into substantial sales dollars.

In a less supportive environment, Steve would not have pursued these entrepreneurial projects. And he would never have realized the tremendous potential he has already displayed in the short time he's been with our company.

Performance Appraisals Under the PGM System

In his book, *The Critical Edge,* Hendrie Weisinger asserts that the major obstacle to a productive performance appraisal is the employee's disagreement with the manager's evaluation. He describes ways to handle such disagreements.[1]

Wouldn't it be nice to prevent disagreements rather than learn how to handle them? That's precisely what the PGM system does. Because performance ratings are tied directly to the accomplishment of goals set by salespeople themselves, there is little room for disputes to arise. The fact that salespeople grade themselves quarterly on their success in achieving goals reduces the likelihood of conflict even further.

These goals account for 80 percent of a sales reps' overall performance rating at the end of the year, which means the reps have a tremendous amount of control over the outcome of their performance reviews. The remaining 20 percent of their rating is based on performance factors (e.g., communication skills, job knowledge).

Performance Ratings

Under the PGM system, salespeople receive one of the following five possible overall performance ratings at their year-end review:

1. *Does not meet expectations:* Consistently fails to meet defined performance goals.
2. *Partially meets expectations:* Infrequently fails to meet one or more important performance goals.

3. *Meets expectations:*   Consistently meets and sometimes exceeds most of the defined performance goals.

4. *Exceeds expectations:*   Exceeds several of the defined goals on a regular basis.

5. *Outstanding:*   Performs at an extraordinary level, based on extremely challenging goals. He or she consistently exceeds at virtually all goals.

In determining a salesperson's rating for the goal section of the performance review (which, as noted earlier, accounts for 80 percent of the total review), consider the mix of Creative and Routine goals set and the range of accomplishment for each goal (Realistic or Dream). The final rating will depend on where the majority of the goals fall, as shown in Figure 3-1.

When the choice of ratings is not clear-cut, consider whether or not quota-related goals were achieved, and if not, whether there was a legitimate reason they were not. Finally, determine whether the person set and met creative goals that address the obstacles that prevented him or her from achieving quota-related goals.

Deriving the Performance Rating: Examples

To see how this system works in practice, let's review two examples, starting with Carl, a sales rep who came in at 103 percent of

Figure 3-1. Performance ratings by goal type and range.

Goal Type*	Range Accomplished*	Performance Rating
Routine	Realistic	Meets expectations
Routine	Dream	Exceeds expectations
Creative	Realistic	Exceeds expectations
Creative	Dream	Outstanding

*Category into which the majority of salesperson's goals fall. If a salesperson fails to achieve the majority of Routine goals in the Realistic range, a rating of "Does not meet expectations" is assigned.

quota for the year. Figure 3-2 summarizes Carl's performance results.

Figure 3-2 shows that eight of the nine goals Carl set are Routine, and the results achieved are within the Realistic range. Because most of Carl's goal achievements fall into the Routine/ Realistic category, his rating will be no higher than "Meets expectations" (see Figure 3-1).

This is an important point, because salespeople who are new to the PGM system sometimes believe they should receive an

Figure 3-2. Summary of Carl's year-end goal results.

Goal (Routine, Creative)	Realistic	Dream	Goal Achieved?
First Quarter			
1. Increase win/loss ratio from 20 percent to X percent (R)	40	60	Yes
2. Meet quarterly number (R)	300	400	Yes
3. Negotiate blanket purchase agreement with ABC Co. to increase quarterly sales from 100k to X in next three quarters (C)	200	300	Yes
Second Quarter			
4. Meet quarterly number (R)	300	400	Yes/Dream
5. Add X prospects to pipeline (R)	20	30	Yes
Third Quarter			
6. Hold key account seminars at all sites to increase sales of product X by X% (R)	20	30	Yes
7. Meet quarterly number (R)	300	400	Yes
Fourth Quarter			
8. Meet quarterly number (R)	300	400	No
9. Add X Prospects to pipeline (R)	30	40	No

overall rating of "Exceeds expectations" just by virtue of the fact that they hit their quotas. But under the PGM system, ratings are not based on quotas met but on goals set and met, and salespeople generally set goals that are more aggressive than their quotas.

Following is another example of how the rating system works. Figure 3-3 shows the year-end performance results of Bob, a sales rep who ended the year at 90 percent of quota.

As Figure 3-3 shows, Bob set four Routine and four Creative goals. He achieved four of the eight goals, including one Creative goal. Since he achieved only half of the goals he set, for this part of the performance review, Bob's rating is on the border between "Partially meets expectations" and "Meets expectations."

Judgment Calls

This is where the sales manager's judgment comes into play. Since Bob came in at just 90 percent of quota, failed to meet a majority of his goals, and met only one of the four Creative goals he set, there is nothing to warrant the higher rating of "Meets expectations." If he had achieved the same number of goals, but more of them were Creative, I would have considered giving him a rating of "Meets expectations" even though he didn't make quota, since the Creative goals would show that he is addressing the obstacles that are preventing him from making quota. The point is, the good judgment of the sales manager is required to assign final ratings effectively in cases that are not clear-cut.

Part of good judgment means determining whether the obstacles to achieving goals are within the salesperson's control. If an obstacle is outside of the control of the salesperson (e.g., a lingering recession), I ask: What Creative goals did the rep set in order to overcome the obstacle and ensure better performance in the future? Reps who achieve such goals should receive a higher performance rating, even if they don't meet quota.

The scenarios above are intended to be used as guidelines in developing your own performance rating system that is tied to a PGM system. It would be impossible to list all of the permutations and combinations of factors that enter into an individual year-end performance rating. The important thing is to develop a system that is as fair and objective as possible.

Figure 3-3. Summary of Bob's year-end goal results.

Goal (Routine, Creative)	Realistic	Dream	Goal Achieved?
First Quarter			
1. Meet quarterly number by maintaining a win/loss ratio of X percent (R)	40%	70%	Yes
2. Create a territory development program to achieve a sales volume of X K per quarter (C)	$350K	$500K	No
Second Quarter			
3. Meet quarterly number by maintaining a win/loss ratio of X percent (R)	40%	70%	Yes
4. Do one educational seminar to increase leads by X per month (C)	3	5	Yes
Third Quarter			
5. Reach 80 percent of sales quota by increasing win/loss ratio to X percent (R)	55%	70%	No
6. Target competitive accounts throughout region to increase overall market share of [product] from 50 percent to X percent (C)	60%	70%	No
Fourth Quarter			
7. Reach 80 percent of annual quota by increasing win/loss ratio to X percent (R)	55%	70%	Yes
8. Target competitive accounts throughout region to increase overall market share of [product] from 50 percent to X percent (C)	60%	70%	No

Performance Factors

Performance factors account for the remaining 20 percent of a salesperson's overall year-end rating. Reps are graded on nine performance factors: communication skills, resourcefulness, job knowledge, development of self and territory, planning, judgment and decisiveness, written communication, teamwork, and productivity.

Performance factors should play a big part in the salesperson's final rating *only* in borderline cases. For example, if a rep is on the border between a rating of "Meets expectations" and "Exceeds expectations," assign the higher rating if the rep is strong in most of the performance factors.

These performance factor ratings are not intended to punish reps but to teach them so that they will be more productive in the future. By discussing your reps' ratings with them at their year-end reviews, they learn what they need to change in order to improve their performance the following year.

Depending on your business and the performance factors you measure, you may want to change the weighting of goals versus performance factors. For example, a new hire who has been on the job for six months or less will not yet be able to develop realistic goals. It's appropriate in that case to give performance factors a greater weight on the year-end review, since those factors will have a great impact on the rep's performance in the long run.

How to Implement a PGM System

Before implementing a Progressive Goal Management system, it's wise to conduct a mini focus group comprised of selected salespeople (no more than five) to give you feedback on the proposed system. Implementation will go more smoothly if you receive feedback from your salespeople during the design stages.

Whomever you choose to include in your PGM system focus group, make sure they are varied. It is most important to include salespeople who think differently than you do. A common pitfall of managers is to ask for feedback only from those employees they know will give instant approval of their plans. This may be the path of least resistance in the short run, but I guarantee that unless you include in your focus group a variety of people with varying opinions, you'll face an uphill struggle to implement and win acceptance of the system.

The focus group I brought together to discuss a proposed PGM system was extremely useful. The members offered a number of excellent suggestions, many of which I incorporated in the final design.

Having people with opposing ideas in the group was particularly useful. One of the first objections to my proposed PGM system came from a salesperson who had a distinctly different philosophy than mine. This rep focuses on the short term rather than thinking strategically. "Why do I have to take the time to write goals every quarter?" he wanted to know.

Listening to this objection, I realized it was possible I would have to play policeman to get in some people's goals on time. I didn't want the PGM system to be painful, so I decided, based on this feedback, to give my reps the following option: if you don't wish to write down your goals each quarter, then your quarterly quota will be your goal.

By incorporating this rule into the system, I deflected any potential objections to turning in quarterly goal lists. I rarely had a rep fail to turn in a goal list. (It's hard to defend not making your quota when you don't have any other goals to show for the quarter.) I would not have thought of this idea were it not for the useful negative comment of one sales rep in the focus group.

Listening to the individual concerns of each member of the focus group helped me prepare for the subsequent twelve individual presentations to the rest of my sales team, since it gave me an indication of the kinds of questions and concerns to expect from them. And it made me feel far more confident that the new PGM system would be successfully implemented and readily accepted.

Managing the Manager's Performance

The success of a Progressive Goal Management system depends on the quality of the sales manager's performance as well as on salespeople's participation. The manager who intends to push salespeople to ever higher levels of achievement should first look in the mirror to determine how effective he or she is as a manager. The quality of the sales manager has a major impact on the success of the sales rep.

Many sales managers unwittingly set up obstacles to their salespeople's performance even as they're pressuring the reps to do better. For example, if the sales manager is a perfectionist who is constantly criticizing his or her reps, those reps will learn to set conservative goals, for fear of failing and being criticized if they set more aggressive or Creative goals.

Earlier in this chapter I noted how my support of Steve enabled him to achieve more aggressive, entrepreneurial goals than he would have pursued on his own. Although my managerial behavior was very helpful to Steve, I was responsible for a team of seventeen salespeople. Perhaps I had a trait that was preventing some of those reps from reaching their full potential. To find out, I periodically asked all my reps to review my performance and let me know where I needed to develop, so that they can improve.

For my development program, I began using a software package called Praxis® (a registered trademark of and published by Acumen International, San Rafael, California). Praxis is a computerized tool to assess and improve managerial skills by pinpointing strengths and weaknesses. The package consists of a 130-question survey on a floppy disk. The survey can be completed at the computer by the manager's direct reports, peers, and/or manager. It takes about twenty to thirty minutes to complete the survey. All input is given anonymously, making it more likely the manager will receive candid responses.

Praxis® looks at the manager's performance in sixteen categories, grouped into four key areas: Task Management, Team Development, Business Values, and Leadership. The complete set of skills measured by the program is shown in Figure 3-4.

After the surveys are completed, the Praxis® program compiles the raw data and generates a consolidated report on the manager's performance, highlighting strengths and pinpointing areas that need improvement.

I distributed the Praxis® disk to four of my direct reports and one of my peers in the company. Figure 3-5 is an excerpt from the consolidated report I received from Praxis®. This section of

Figure 3-4. Outline of PRAXIS skill areas.

Task Management:	Defining work activities, providing the task structure necessary for results
	■ Informing ■ Efficiency ■ Planning ■ Problem Solving
Team Development:	Providing people with the motivation and supportive social climate required for long-term high levels of performance and satisfaction
	■ Performance Feedback ■ Relationship Skills ■ Staff Development ■ Team Motivation
Business Values:	Measures the broad strategic choices that managers make in the values and business operations they promote
	■ Quality Improvement ■ Customer Focus ■ Promoting Innovation
Leadership:	Demonstrating the personal skills that enhance a manager's ability to motivate and direct the actions of others
	■ Accountability ■ Empowerment ■ Influence ■ Mission Skills ■ Networking

Reprinted with permission of Acumen International, San Rafael, California.

the report, Item-Level Feedback, shows the range of responses I received in the areas of Informing and Efficiency.

Item-Level Feedback is especially helpful in identifying managerial trouble spots. Although my final scores for each skill were quite satisfactory, there was one area, Promoting Innovation, in which the responses from five of my direct reports were spread out over a wide range, signalling that there might be a problem in that skill area.

For areas where there is a range of responses, the program explains the possible reasons. In the area of promoting innova-

Figure 3-5. Item-level feedback.

ITEM-LEVEL FEEDBACK

The discussion of each skill area will show you how your co-workers rated you on each of the items measuring that skill area. For example, here is how your co-workers describe you on one of the items in Informing:

- Provides a steady, reliable flow of information to the team

The scale at the top of the display is what your co-workers used in making the ratings, 1 ("Never") to 5 ("Always"). The length of the shaded horizontal bar shows your average rating from co-workers. The black vertical stripe shows the results of the average manager in the norm group. For example, on the item displayed here, the average score in the norm group is about 3.8, and you can see that your co-workers rated you near this point. Therefore, it is clear that your score from co-workers is about average on this item.

You may notice that these dark vertical stripes are seldom centered near "3.0" on the five-point scale; they are usually closer to the high end of the scale, meaning that an average manager has good skills. In effect, your skills are compared to a high standard.

Here is another example of feedback about a specific item. This item is from the Efficiency skill area and this time it describes a counterproductive behavior:

- Gets distracted by tangential issues

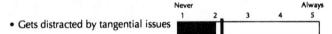

An ideal manager would be described as "Never" doing this behavior. For "counterproductive " behaviors, a longer shaded bar shows a higher level of undesired behavior— and less skill.

On this particular item, the horizontal bar showing your results extends to a point near the black vertical stripe showing the average manager's score; therefore, you can see that your results are about average on this item.

HOW TO USE THIS FEEDBACK

How you use this information is up to you. By design, the separately detailed feedback about specific skill areas allows you to find and read about the skills of most interest to you, perhaps skimming over the others.

Examining the results shown for each item may help you get a much better understanding of how co-workers describe your skills. These results may give you some good ideas about activities you could do more often or more effectively.

Reprinted with permission of Acumen International, San Rafael, California.

Figure 3-6. "Empowerment" results.

The <u>Empowerment</u> scale measures your tendency to push decision-making authority and responsibility downward, giving team members "ownership" of their work. This goes beyond merely assigning tasks: You empower team members by demonstrating faith in them to take complete charge within their sphere of operation. This means clearly communicating confidence in their abilities and making them responsible for solving the problems they encounter.

YOUR RESULTS
Your results are shown here for each of the items that measure Empowerment. Your score from co-workers is shown by the length of the shaded area. A dark vertical stripe marks the score of an average manager. You can see exactly what co-workers say about how well you help them feel empowered.

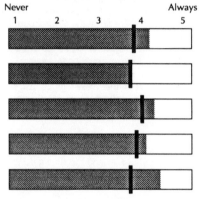

- Delegates in a way that uses others' talents effectively
- Empowers others to take charge
- Encourages others to take responsibility
- Gives public recognition to others' contributions; shares the limelight
- Shows confidence in others by letting them make important decisions

The following item describes a counterproductive tendency, so a better score is one that is <u>lower</u> than the average manager's:

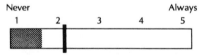

- Has difficulty letting others have full control of their work

On the whole, you scored highest in these Empowerment categories. As the graphic shows, co-workers regard your Empowerment skills as higher than that of many other managers.

Managers with your Empowerment skills tend to make team members feel as if they can and should be taking complete responsibility within their defined areas. Co-workers feel very accountable for even small actions and feel a sense of confidence that they can, indeed, achieve the desired results. They always feel comfortable that you will treat their taking of responsibility as the right thing to do, and they look forward to your public acknowledgment of their role.

tion, my results suggested that I may have been encouraging innovation in some people but not in others.

When I thought about the results, I realized it was possible that I viewed some people as more creative than others and may not have tried to promote innovation with all of my reps. That would explain the spread among the five responses.

Promoting innovation is a crucial skill for the manager who wants to encourage reps to set Creative goals. To make sure I strengthened my ability in this area, I developed an action plan to make sure I encourage all of my salespeople to be innovative.

Fortunately, I received my highest score in the area of Empowerment, a key skill for promoting self-management.

Figure 3-6, an excerpt from the body of the Praxis® report, shows my results in this area.

After identifying areas of managerial weakness, it's a good idea to discuss the results with your salespeople and ask for their input on how you can improve. And to make sure you continue to progress, have your employees and peers review you every six months or so, using Praxis® or another system.

Finally, to get the most out of a development tool such as Praxis®, it's important to overcome any defensiveness about being reviewed by your employees or peers. This assessment tool is not intended to be used as a weapon against you, but as a way of helping you develop your managerial potential.

Note

1. Hendrie Weisinger, *The Critical Edge* (Boston: Little, Brown, 1989), Chapter 8.

Chapter 4

Macro and Micro Sales Management

Sales management planning can be divided into two categories: macro and micro management. *Macro management* involves analyzing economic forecasts, the political climate, the competition, industry trends, capacity utilization figures, new legal rulings and other broad "macro" factors that may have an impact on sales in a given territory. *Micro management* involves monitoring salespeoples' activities and developing strategies and tools to help them become more effective in the macro environment.

The choice of micro management tools and strategies will vary according to conditions in the macro environment. For example, as the task force headed by Hillary Rodham Clinton was preparing a proposal on health care reform in 1993, even before anyone knew the details of the ultimate plan for reform, they knew that cost containment was sure to be a central aspect of it.

With tighter controls on testing and lower reimbursements (two likely outcomes of reform), the demand for testing equipment will decline and the payback period will increase, making equipment purchases harder for physicians and hospitals to justify. The sales manager must be aware of such eventualities and develop the micro management tools to deal with them. In this example, physicians and hospitals might be given the option of leasing rather than buying equipment in order to reduce their financial exposure.

The macro factors that influence the micro environment of the salesperson can change from month to month, and even from day to day. It is the sales manager's job to keep track of these changes and to help the salesperson adjust to them quickly and effectively.

Macro Management Tools

There are variety of macro management tools the sales manager can use to analyze a sales territory, including commercial and retail databases, software mapping programs, industry associations, and business newspapers.

Commercial and Retail Databases

One way to get an objective picture of a sales territory is by tapping into a commercial or retail database. Commercial databases provide general information about businesses, such as type of products, level of annual sales, and number of employees. Retail databases provide demographic information about individuals and households, such as age, income, and race or ethnicity. If you know the profile of your typical buyer (discussed in Chapter 5), you can tap these databases to find new customers who match the profile.

Most databases are available in a variety of formats, including magnetic tape, index cards, and computer diskette, which enables the user to plug the data directly into a spreadsheet program. You can even download many databases directly to your computer if you have a modem. Once the data are loaded into a spreadsheet, you can sort the records to get a quick profile of existing and potential accounts in a territory.

List Compilers vs. List Brokers. There are two types of database vendors: *list compilers*, who create the data, and *list brokers*, who buy and resell (or, more commonly, rent) the compiled lists. List compilers are less expensive to use, but you have to know where to find them (a good reference librarian can help).

List brokers have access to a wide range of lists; it's better to use them if you don't know which companies/compilers might be the best suppliers of the information you need.

Defining Information Requirements. Whether you use a compiler or a broker, you'll achieve better results if you define your information requirements in as much detail as possible. Following is an example of criteria you might give to a list compiler or broker if you wanted to do a broad search to find new customers within the manufacturing sector.

Annual sales volume	$5 million to 50 million
Zip codes:	93600 through 96899 (northern California)
SIC codes:	2000 through 3699 (manufacturing companies)

The longer the SIC code, the narrower the search. For example, if you want to target the electronics industry, or a subsegment of the industry, you might ask for a search within a five-, six-, or seven-digit SIC code, depending on how carefully you have defined your target market.

It's important to specify what types of facilities you want to search for (e.g., headquarters, branch offices, sales offices). You should also specify, by title, who within the company you wish to contact (e.g., vice president of purchasing). If the compiler or broker cannot find an exact match for this title, ask for the title of someone higher up in the organization who is likely to know the person you wish to contact (e.g., the vice president of manufacturing or the plant manager can likely direct you to the head of purchasing).

If you are in a retail business, before you rush to a list compiler or broker with your general criteria, review the "Survey of Buying Power" published by *Sales and Marketing Management Magazine*, in each September issue. The survey provides a wide range of consumer demographic information, such as population by age group, income level, and race or ethnicity, for major metropolitan areas, states, and regions of the country. By comparing the survey results to your buyer profile, you can determine which geographic markets have the highest concentration of potential customers. This will enable you to narrow the focus of your search before you approach a compiler or broker, saving you time and money.

For example, if your products are most often bought by people in the twenty to thirty-five age group, you may find a higher concentration of prospective customers in Southern California. If you sell to senior citizens, Florida might be a better market for you.

Let the Buyer Beware. It's critical that you find out how often the contact names in a database are verified by telephone. Professional list compilers may have millions of companies verified every year for accuracy. Less professional firms may do less frequent checks. You should select only databases whose information is verified at least once a year. With the cost of a salesperson's face-to-face selling time currently ranging from $250 to $300 per hour, you cannot afford to have a rep pursuing retired or deceased contacts.

Unfortunately, you don't always know what you're getting from a list compiler or broker, even when you ask. I learned this lesson the hard way.

When I first started as a sales manager, I acquired from a list compiler a database of all manufacturing facilities in my assigned region. I wanted to get a handle on the market potential of each of my reps' territories.

I had the reps contact all of the accounts in their territories by phone to identify the best prospects. They quickly discovered that quite a few of the locations listed in the database were branch offices or sales offices rather than manufacturing facilities and that the contact names were old.

The moral of the story: Make sure that you deal with a credible list compiler or broker who has a good reputation within the industry. To find out which companies have the best reputation, ask colleagues who have made use of these services in the past, and talk to people within the industry. The quality of compilers and brokers varies dramatically, so let the buyer beware.

Software Mapping Programs

Earlier I noted that you can plug your database information directly into a spreadsheet program. If you use the spreadsheet with a software mapping program,[1] you can get a visual image of how your accounts and prospects are spread out over a territory.

The popular commercial mapping programs contain regional and metropolitan atlases. If the records in your database include zip codes, this information can be used to generate a computerized map of a sales territory, such as the one shown in Figure 4-1.

Through the use of color variations or patterns of various shades, the mapping program will enable you to differentiate areas of high customer concentration from low ones, or to highlight other aspects of the sales territory (Figure 4-2). These capabilities make it easier for you to help salespeople who are having trouble managing their territories effectively.

For example, one of my scientific instrument sales reps, Sharon, was spending too much of her time on low-potential accounts, and not enough time in high-potential areas. Together, we developed a territory profile, using mapping software, so that Sharon could easily see which areas she should be targeting.

We divided Sharon's territory into four geographic pockets, using a mapping program. Then we compared the percentage share of potential business in each pocket with the proportion of time Sharon spent on each, as shown below.

As Figure 4-3 indicates, Sharon was spending about the right percentage of her time in Pockets C and D. But she was spending too much time in B and not enough in A, relative to their sales potential. With this new information, Sharon adjusted her priorities and allocated her selling time more productively.

The next step was for Sharon to determine the breakdown of accounts within each pocket. Sharon sold primarily to hospitals. Using database information and a spreadsheet, she was able to sort her hospital account records by number of beds or according to whether or not the hospitals have an intensive care unit, to separate large from small facilities.

Once she categorized the hospitals by size, with the help of a spreadsheet program, she was able to develop more targeted selling strategies. For example, she determined to focus on selling lower cost products via direct mail to small hospitals with limited budgets and restrict face-to-face visits to large hospitals with the potential to purchase expensive products.

(Text continues on page 66)

Figure 4-1. Software-generated sales territory map.

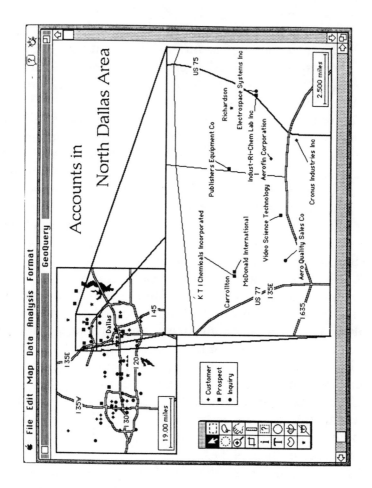

Figure 4-2. Territory breakout.

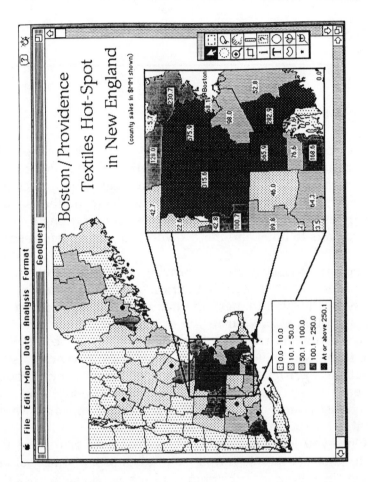

Figure 4-3. Market share vs. actual time spent.

Territory	% Share of Total Market	% Actual Time Spent
Pocket A	45	30
Pocket B	30	41
Pocket C	15	17
Pocket D	10	12

Industry Associations

Another useful tool for gathering macro information is the industry association. If you are trying to penetrate a particular industry or business segment and if it's a large enough segment, chances are there is an association representing it. There are thousands of industry associations in the United States, representing everyone from bankers to hotel and motel owners to pharmaceutical scientists.

Industry associations can provide you with excellent, fast information about specific industries. Association meetings are an easy way for you to meet and talk with people who represent the key industries in your region or territory. If you want to get an idea of industry trends or learn more about your competitors, strike up a conversation with a member or two. You can also get immediate feedback from association members about products and services your company offers or plans to develop. And if you are seriously interested in cracking a market, you may want to exhibit in an upcoming association trade show.

Once you join an association (annual dues can range from $250 to $1,000 or more), you can take advantage of other valuable services including membership directories. Some associations mail newsletters to their members, which usually include a calendar of upcoming events and announcements of promotions of movers and shakers within the industry.

For a comprehensive list of associations, consult *The Encyclopedia of Associations*, available in any major library. This annual directory provides detailed information about national and international associations, including names of executive officers, membership numbers, dues, publications, activities, and such. There are alphabetical and geographic indexes, as a well as a "key word index," that will help you to find all of the associations connected to a specific industry.

Business Newspapers

Most major metropolitan areas have a weekly business newspaper that covers events and trends pertaining to local companies and industries. For example, in San Francisco it is the *San Francisco Business Times*.

By subscribing to these newspapers, you can keep current on which sectors of the local economy are prospering or declining, which businesses are succeeding or failing, and what your competition is doing. These papers usually include a "People on the Move" section which, along with association newsletters, will help you to keep track of the movers and shakers within various companies and industries.

For even more targeted news, subscribe to industry-specific tabloids, which can be found in virtually every region of the country. These newspapers often include economic indexes of their industry, important information that is not usually found in general business newspapers.

Micro Management Tools

Once the macro environment is analyzed, the sales manager must develop micro management tools to ensure that salespeople are using their time wisely and responding effectively to the changing conditions in their territories. Following are examples of some effective micro management tools.

The Daily Contact Report

The Daily Contact Report tracks the face-to-face calls a salesperson makes on a given day. At a minimum, the Daily Contact Report should include the following information about each sales call:

- Date
- Company name and address
- Contact name and title
- Space for comments

You might add some additional fields to the report, so that your reps can record the sources of leads, customer reactions to various products, prices and promotions, the probability of closing the order, or any other information that might be useful to the sales or marketing department. The information you decide to collect should be determined by the specific goals you want to achieve. For instance, if you are selling a new product and are not quite sure of the demographics of the typical buyer, you might want to gather detailed information about prospects who show interest in the product. A sample Daily Contact Report is shown in Figure 4-4. (This particular report also includes space for the sales rep to report on product demos.)

For the sales manager in a new territory that has inadequate historical records, the Daily Contact Report can be used to gather information quickly about the profile of the territory. Another advantage is that the report enables the sales manager and the salesperson to respond quickly to events at a particular account.

Suppose the Daily Contact Report of one of your reps shows that a quote was sent to XYZ Company on the first of May. If you know that an order usually follows four weeks after a quote is sent, you can track the progress of the sale and determine when it's time for you to step in and coach the rep to close the order.

Weekly Call Report

The Weekly Call Report (Figure 4-5) provides an overview of the salesperson's activities during the previous week. This report should include the name and address of the company, date of each call, and objectives accomplished. This last item will help you to determine whether the rep is making high-impact calls or just passing the time. You might also reserve space at the bottom of the report to record total calls for the week, number of product demonstrations made, number of leads followed up, number of

Figure 4-4. Daily contact report.

	Check Applicable Box
Test Instruments Division **Demonstration** **& Contact Report** If Phone Contact, Check ☐	☐ Oscilloscope (Model # _____) ☐ 500 ☐ Other

Sales Engineer _____ Date _____

Name _____ Others Attending _____

Company _____ _____

Dept. _____ _____

Address _____ _____

City _____ _____

State _____ Zip _____ _____

Phone _____ Ext _____ _____

Source of Contact ☐ Bingo ☐ Show ☐ Call Cold ☐ Customer Reference ☐ NIC User ☐ Mailing ☐ Other

Application _____

_____

_____

_____

_____

How Did the Demo Go? _____

_____

_____

_____

_____

Next Contact Date _____ Competition _____ Probability of Order (%) _____

Demo Left: ☐ Yes ☐ No   Preparing Quote: ☐ Yes ☐ No   Mail List: ☐ Add ☐ Delete ☐ Change

Follow-Up Plan _____

_____

Comments _____

_____

_____

_____

_____

_____

White Copy • Madison   Yellow Copy • Regional Manager   Pink Copy • Sales Engineer

Figure 4-5. Weekly call report.

Name _____

Week ending _____

Sales this week	27,825	# of on-site calls	
Month to date	27,825	# of demonstrations	
Goal for month	65K	# leads followed up	
Quarter to date	47,815	# of lost sales	
Goal for quarter	175K		

DAY	ACCOUNT NAME	ID	LOCATION	OBJECTIVES ACCOMPLISHED
SUN				
MON 3				
TUES 4				
WED 5				
THURS 6				
FRI 7				
SAT				

COMMENTS:
☐ Sales Management   ☐ Product Management   ☐ Administration   ☐ Field Service
☐ New Product Ideas   ☐ Competitive Activity   ☐ Other

TO BE COMPLETED AND MAILED BY THE END OF EACH WEEK WITH
EXPENSE REPORT

White-Sales Rep   Yellow-Regional Sales Manager   Pink-National Sales Manager lost sales, and any other information that will help you to track and improve the rep's performance.

The Weekly Call Report is especially useful for salespeople who have trouble managing their time effectively. By providing a detailed record of how many hours they are devoting to selling, this report can help salespeople to spot time management problems and learn how to allocate their work hours more effectively.

Monthly Itinerary

The Monthly Itinerary (Figure 4-6) is an excellent planning tool for the rep who spends a good deal of time (perhaps, 30 percent or more) traveling and whose accounts are spread out over a large territory. This report, which is prepared during the last week of the month for the following month, helps the salesperson and the sales manager to ensure that no territory is being over- or under-visited.

In the absence of a planning tool such as the Monthly Itinerary, it's all too easy for the rep to schedule too many visits to nearby or desirable locations and too few trips to tough accounts or less desirable areas. The Monthly Itinerary helps the rep to avoid this temptation.

Won/Lost Report

The Won/Lost Report (Figure 4-7) details the outcome of every proposed sale. This is one of the most critical reports a company produces. Not only does it enable the sales manager to identify selling obstacles and help the rep to overcome them, but it provides marketing personnel and product managers with the information they need to create effective new strategies or modify existing ones. The fields for this report include:

- Company name and address
- Contact name and title
- Competitor name (for the particular product being sold)
- Product model
- Product price
- Reason for loss or win

Figure 4-6. Monthly itinerary.

Monthly Planning Form

Name: _____
Month: __JUNE__

Sat./Sun.	Monday	Tuesday	Wednesday	Thursday	Friday
1 2	3	4	5	6	7
8 9	10	11	12	13	14
15 16	17	18	19	20	21
22 23	24	25	26	27	28
29 30					

Most important things to be done this month:

1. _____
2. _____
3. _____

4. _____
5. _____
6. _____

Itinerary should include name and location of key accounts, prospects, and meetings.

Figure 4-7. Won/lost report.

Date Order Won/Lost:		Salesperson:			
Company:					
Customer Name:		Telephone:			
Address:					
City:		State:		Zip:	

Competitor:	Model:	Price:	Model:	Price:

Reason for Loss or Win:

You might also leave space for reps to record information about competitors' strategies that might negatively affect your business (e.g., promotions offering deep discounts, or the development of new products or product features).

It's good to have salespeople report the details of how orders were won, especially if they used creative tactics to get the business, so that their colleagues can benefit from their experience. In my company, we send Won/Lost reports to corporate headquarters, where they are compiled, summarized, and distributed to the field. This information enables reps to copy the successful strategies of their colleagues and to gather important information (e.g., a competitor in one territory who is about to move into theirs) that will help them respond to competitive threats.

If salespeople are consistently losing out to competitors, it's a good idea for them to visit key competitor accounts to learn what the customer likes about the competitor and where improvement is needed. This information should then be communicated to the marketing department, so that product and marketing strategies can be adjusted.

The Twelve-Month Revolving Operations Forecast

The Twelve-Month Revolving Operations Forecast shows the number and dollar amount of orders a salesperson expects to close within the next thirty, sixty, or ninety days and beyond, up to twelve months. The forecast includes the following information fields:

- Name of salesperson
- Name and address of account (or prospect)
- Contact person and title
- Product type
- Dollar amount of prospective sale
- Time frame—30, 60, 90 or "Prospect" (up to 12 months)
- Status
- Comments

The status field is used to indicate whether an order has a high or low probability of closing within a certain time frame. An account is labeled "high probability" only when the sale is virtually certain to occur in the given time period.

The Twelve-Month Revolving Forecast serves three purposes. It helps the company to determine short-term inventory requirements, by showing the number and type of orders that will be generated within the next thirty, sixty, and ninety days. It serves as a revenue forecast for the coming year. It helps the sales manager to determine which reps are in need of closer management, based on the number and size of prospects in various stages of the pipeline.

A simple rule of thumb is that the rep should have a minimum of 2.5 times more legitimate business (high probability orders) in the twelve-month pipeline than his or her quota. I emphasize the word "legitimate" because salespeople, especially those in a slump, tend to become victims of wishful thinking.

People who go into sales tend to be optimistic by nature. This optimism can easily turn into denial when they are in a sales slump. Then, they may begin to see even long shots as likely prospects and lull themselves into a false sense of security. To prevent this from happening, the sales manager must conduct frequent "reality checks" with salespeople, to ensure that the prospects in their pipeline are truly viable.

The Three-Year Prospect Report

The Three-Year Prospect Report shows sales in the pipeline that are expected to close within the next 36 months. It includes the same basic fields as the Twelve-Month Revolving Forecast: name of salesperson, company name and address of account (or prospect), contact person and title, product type, dollar amount of prospective sale, and comments.

You may want to add fields to indicate the industry or type of business and how leads were generated. This information will help you to identify shifts in buying patterns and determine where extra selling effort may be required. By tracking the percentage conversion of prospective sales to hard orders from different stages in the pipeline, you can help your salespeople to improve their prospecting skills. And by tracking leads through to closed orders, you can determine the most lucrative sources of leads and use this information to help reps improve their prospecting skills.

If you begin to implement one or more of the reporting tools described above without communicating the purpose of the tool to your salespeople, they may suspect you have a hidden agenda, that you are trying to spy on them. As a result, they may stop communicating with you; at the very least, they will begin to censor their communications. You cannot afford to let this happen, as these reports are crucial to effective planning and management, not just for the sales manager but for other departments.

Automating Micro Management

With the price of computer technology declining every day, even small companies can automate the sales reports described above. There are several software packages now on the market that are specifically designed for salespeople. These "contact software programs" make it easy to combine and manipulate the information gathered in these reports. Once you have developed a format or template on a contact software program, the raw data can be summarized and manipulated to produce a variety of other reports.

In setting up the template, it's necessary to determine all of the information you want to gather for sales management, marketing, and any other purposes. At a minimum, you should plan on collecting all the information needed for the reports outlined above.

Figure 4-8 shows a typical layout for a computerized contact report. Depending on your own company's sales and marketing goals, you may want to include other fields specific to your business, as noted earlier. For example, Figure 4-8 includes an optional field to track the last order date, so that a sales rep can be alerted to any account that falls behind the normal order pattern.

Figure 4-9 shows an activity report that was generated from the contact report. This activity report gives the sales manager and rep a snapshot profile of the account's history and notes.

Figure 4-10 shows how the sales rep can merge all the information from the contact report into a personalized thank you letter, with the help of a word processing package that comes with the contact software.

The amount of time saved by using an automated system is substantial. Without automation, the same account information may be entered by your salespeople on one form or another three or more times in a single month. With an automated system that is set up properly, with all reports linked, once a piece of information is entered into the system, it never has to be entered again. And when information is updated on one report, it is automatically updated on all linked reports.

Macro and Micro Management: Application Examples

The following examples show how macro and micro management tools are applied in various sales situations. These examples

(Text continues on page 80)

Figure 4-8. Computerized contact report.

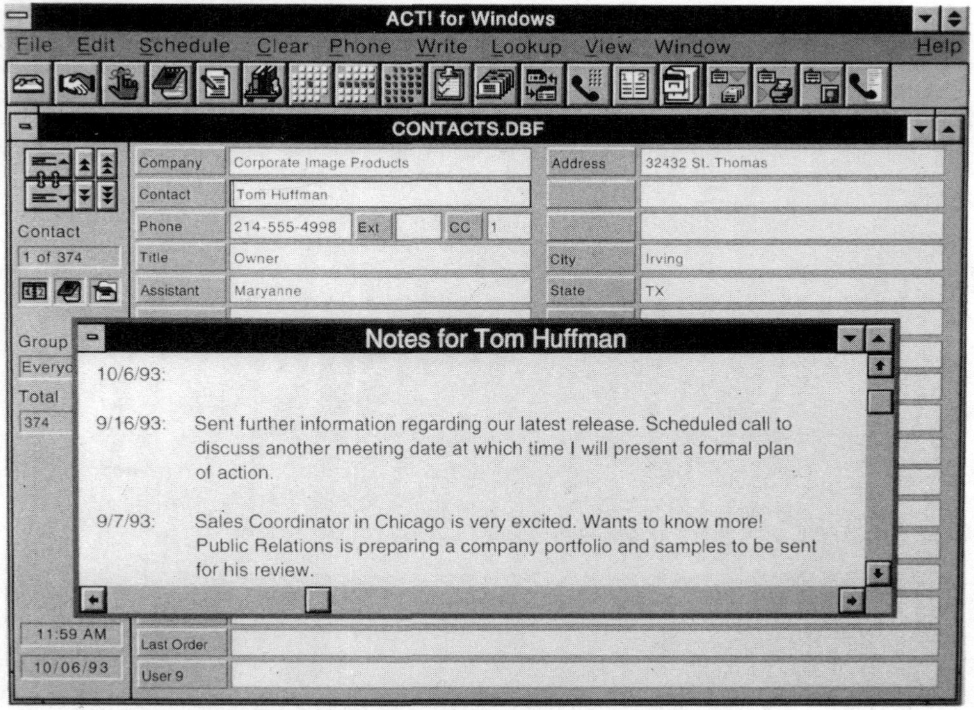

Produced on ACT! software. Reprinted with permission of Symantec Corporation, Cupertino, California.

Figure 4-9. Computerized activity report.

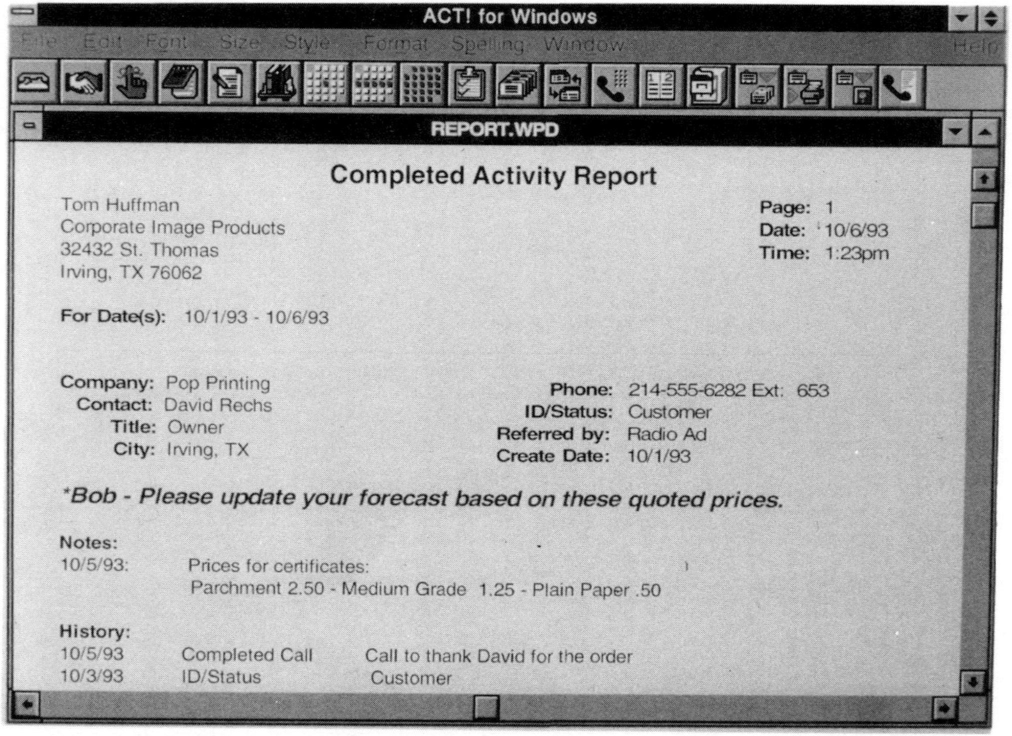

ACT! for Windows

File Edit Font Size Style Format Spelling Window

REPORT.WPD

Completed Activity Report

Tom Huffman
Corporate Image Products
32432 St. Thomas
Irving, TX 76062

Page: 1
Date: 10/6/93
Time: 1:23pm

For Date(s): 10/1/93 - 10/6/93

Company: Pop Printing
Contact: David Rechs
Title: Owner
City: Irving, TX

Phone: 214-555-6282 Ext: 653
ID/Status: Customer
Referred by: Radio Ad
Create Date: 10/1/93

Bob - Please update your forecast based on these quoted prices.

Notes:
10/5/93:   Prices for certificates:
            Parchment 2.50 - Medium Grade 1.25 - Plain Paper .50

History:
10/5/93   Completed Call   Call to thank David for the order
10/3/93   ID/Status   Customer

Produced on ACT! software. Reprinted with permission of Symantec Corporation, Cupertino, California.

Figure 4-10. Automated thank you letter.

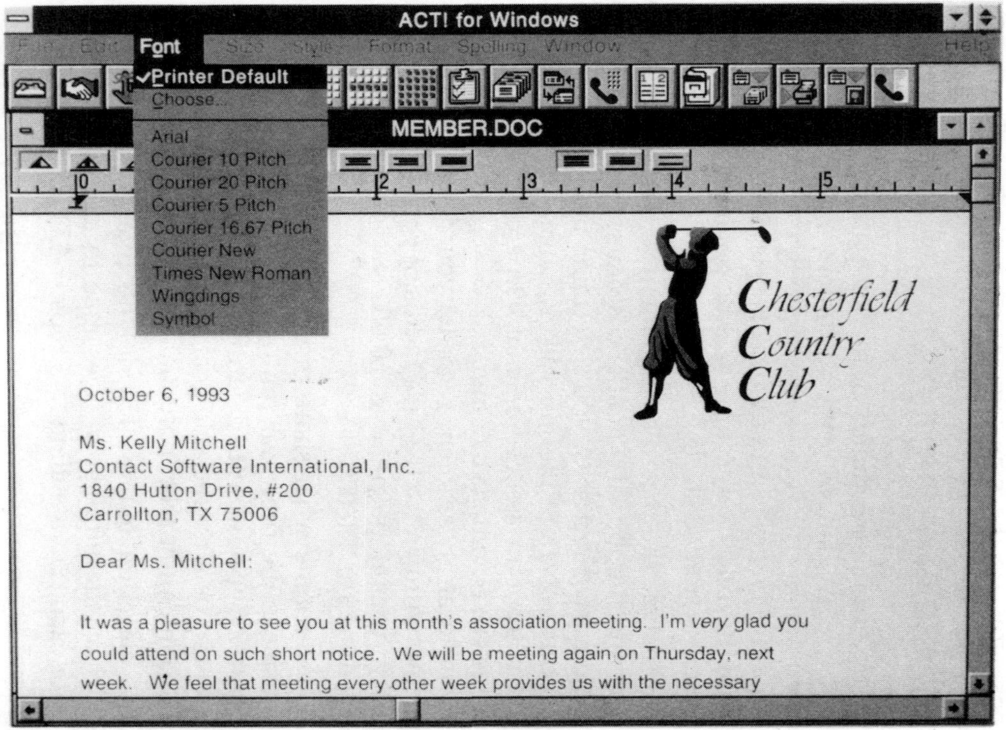

ACT! for Windows

Font — Printer Default — Choose...

Arial
Courier 10 Pitch
Courier 20 Pitch
Courier 5 Pitch
Courier 16.67 Pitch
Courier New
Times New Roman
Wingdings
Symbol

MEMBER.DOC

Chesterfield Country Club

October 6, 1993

Ms. Kelly Mitchell
Contact Software International, Inc.
1840 Hutton Drive, #200
Carrollton, TX 75006

Dear Ms. Mitchell:

It was a pleasure to see you at this month's association meeting. I'm *very* glad you could attend on such short notice. We will be meeting again on Thursday, next week. We feel that meeting every other week provides us with the necessary reflect common scenarios that most sales managers face every day.

Scenario 1: Establishing Sales Quotas

Suppose you are the new owner of a waterbed store, and you want to assign quotas to your salespeople. To establish fair quotas, you will have to go through the following process:

1. Determine the radius of market potential from the store, based on conversations with customers, the location of other waterbed stores and your own shopping experience. You determine that twelve miles in any direction is potential for business. Anything beyond twelve miles will be potential for closer, more convenient waterbed stores.

2. Analyze the macro environment to determine the demographics and number of potential customers in your market area. From industry directories, you determine that people ages eighteen to thirty-five are the most likely buyers of waterbeds, and you learn from an association that 40 percent of people in this age range are potential customers.

From local government records, you determine that 60,000 people live within a twelve-mile radius of your store. So, the total market (revenue) potential is 60,000 × .4 × $700 (price per waterbed) = $16,800,000.

3. Determine what share of the market is reasonable for a new business the first year and multiply the total potential by this figure. Suppose you determine that a 10 percent market share would be a respectable goal your first year. This translates to a $1.68 million market potential.

4. Determine quotas: Divide the total amount of market potential by the number of sales reps to determine the annual quota for each ($1.68 million ÷ 5 reps = $336,000 quota per rep).

Scenario 2: Determining the Source of Slumping Sales

When sales numbers are low, it's tempting for sales managers to look for a quick fix, such as putting a rep on a ninety-day probation. A better approach is to determine the source of the problem first, by using macro and micro tools.

The four most likely causes of a decline in overall sales in a territory or region are:

1. An excessive amount of business lost to the competition
2. A shortage of prospects in the pipeline
3. Poor territory management
4. Depressed economic conditions

The sales manager must evaluate each of these possible factors to determine which is the true source of the sales slump.

It's easy to determine if the problem stems from business lost to the competition (item 1). Simply review the Won/Lost reports for the territory or region and determine the won/lost ratio for each salesperson.

If a salesperson's ratio is below the benchmark (i.e., the ratio a given sales rep can reasonably be expected to achieve, based on conditions in the territory), you must identify the cause of the poor performance. If the rep's ratio is below that of his or her colleagues, additional coaching may be all that it takes to improve performance.

If all the reps' ratios are below the benchmark, the problem could lie with the product. Perhaps it is not appropriately priced, or is missing a competitive feature. In that case, all you can do is take up the issue with the folks in marketing and product development.

It could be that depressed economic conditions are causing customers to become more price-sensitive, and this is resulting in a greater percentage of lost sales. If so, this is a problem that the marketing department must address.

To determine whether a sales slump is the result of a shortage of prospects in the pipeline (item 2), use the simple rule outlined above. Make sure there is 2.5 times more sales potential in the twelve-month pipeline than the sales rep's quota.

If it turns out that a salesperson is not putting enough business into the pipeline, you must look at the possible causes. One of the most common causes is inadequate time spent in territory development.

Following are some immediate steps you can have the rep take to build up the pipeline: networking, referrals, free presentations to local associations and clubs, cold telephone calls, direct mail, advertising, seminars, articles in business magazines, and business section of the newspaper.

It's important to try a combination of tactics rather than rely on one or two. With time and persistence, the sales rep will succeed in building the pipeline to an acceptable level.

It's also important that the rep pursues those sources that will generate the highest return on his or her investment of time. This requires that the rep knows which prospects are the strongest and how they conduct business.

For example, people in the biotechnology industry have told me they don't have time to attend general trade shows, but they do go to their own association meetings. The best place to meet them is probably at their association meetings. (Incidentally, if you are unsure of the best avenues to reach your prospects, get on the phone and ask. In my experience, people are generally forthcoming with this type of information.)

If you have not yet uncovered the source of the sales downturn, it could be that a sales rep is not managing his or her territory effectively (item 3). For example, if the demographics show that the highest potential for territorial growth is the food industry and your sales rep is doing little to cultivate business in this industry, that could be the problem.

To determine whether poor territory management is the source of the problem, use mapping software to compare the location of potential customers in the territory to the territory being covered by your rep, based on information from the Twelve-Month Forecast. You will quickly see whether or not the rep is overlooking a high-potential geographic area.

If all else fails, the problem may rest in the macro environment. For example, slumping sales may be due to nothing more than a poor economy.

It's not too difficult to get economic news. Simply review business newspapers, industry magazines, or association newsletters and talk to industry sources to determine which business segments are prospering and which are faltering. Use this news as a compass to guide your salespeople's day-to-day activities in the right direction.

It may be that a combination of factors is responsible for the decline in sales. You must determine whether these factors will have a temporary or permanent effect before you take action to counter them. For example, an economic downturn and poor territory management may be causing the decline. If you feel that the economy will improve in the near future, coaching your sales rep in territory development would be a good move. However, if the economic downturn is likely to be permanent, all the territory development in the world won't do you any good, and you will have to seek out new markets for your products, or develop new products for economically healthier markets.

Scenario 3: Improving Time and Territory Management

Following is a more detailed, step-by-step example of how you would apply micro and macro management tools to help a sales rep, Ellen, who is performing below quota due to poor time and territory management.

How to Apply Micro and Macro Management Tools

1. *Analyze the sales territory by market sector.* First, analyze the makeup of Ellen's sales territory by market sector with the help of a commercial database. The major market sectors for Ellen's products (scientific equipment) are industry, universities, and government. From the database, determine the composition of Ellen's territory and compare it to the breakdown of her accounts, as reflected in her Twelve-Month Revolving Forecast. If she is managing her territory effectively, you would expect the percentages to be roughly equivalent.

Figure 4-11 shows that Ellen is doing a good job of covering industry and university business, but could be spending more time developing government accounts.

2. *Analyze market segments within major market sectors.* Compare the percentage of Ellen's accounts in the Industry sector of

Figure 4-11. Sales territory by market sector.

	Market Potential	Ellen's Accounts	Opportunity Spread
Industry	53%	56%	-3%
University	26	30	-4
Government	21	14	7

her territory, which can be subdivided into three segments: chemicals, electronics, and biotechnology. They should parallel the percentages of potential business in each segment.

From Figure 4-12 we can see that although Ellen is spending about the right amount of time overall in developing Industry accounts, there is more potential in the chemicals and electronics industry than she is mining.

3. *Analyze the macro environment to determine the outlook for individual market segments.* Before determining whether Ellen should spend more time developing government, chemical, and electronics accounts, you must look at each of these segments more closely to determine whether the near-term outlook for these segments justifies additional sales development activity.

From an external database, you know there are two major companies that make up close to 50 percent of the chemical industry segment in Ellen's territory. You also know that one of these companies is shutting down some of its labs and consolidating its facilities in the Midwest. The other company has been affected by declining profits and is limiting its spending to investments with a short payback period. This means that growth in the chemical industry is likely to be stagnant in this territory in the foreseeable future.

The outlook in the electronics segment is mixed. New semiconductor plants are being built in other regions of the country and in Asia. The only chance for growth in Ellen's territory is in the replacement market; some customers will be replacing their old equipment with new, PC-driven products during the new three years.

The outlook in the biotechnology market is strong. Three

Figure 4-12. Breakdown of industry segments.

	Percentage of Total Market (Macro World)	Percentage of Ellen's Accounts (Micro World)	Opportunity Spread
Total	53%	55%	2%
Chemicals	38	15	23
Electronics	30	14	16
Biotechnology	24	26	-2

prominent university research centers promoting biotechnology are located in Ellen's territory. Scientific equipment sales to these centers are expected to grow, since the National Science Foundation and other grant-giving institutions are replacing aged equipment with new products. Furthermore, the FDA is starting to relax its bureaucratic approval of new products, giving the biotech marketplace further impetus for growth from existing facilities and the startup of new biotech facilities.

From this analysis, you conclude that Ellen should maintain her emphasis in the area of biotechnology. She should also pursue the replacement market segment of the electronic industry. But she should continue to de-emphasize the rest of the electronics industry and the chemical industry, since the outlook for these segments is weak.

4. *Analyze the pipeline.* The next step is to analyze Ellen's pipeline, with the help of the Three-Year Prospect Report. From this report, you see that Ellen has 11 percent of the pipeline in the ninety-day category, another 33 percent occurring beyond ninety days, within the next twelve months. The remaining 55 percent are "suspects"—accounts expected to close beyond twelve months, but still within the three-year time frame. Ellen's pipeline distribution is shown in Figure 4-13.

A good rule of thumb is to have *at least* 10 percent of potential revenues in the thirty-to-ninety day segment of the pipeline; 25 percent in the four-to-twelve-month segment, and 65 percent in the one-to-three-year portion of the pipeline.

Figure 4-13. Pipeline distribution.

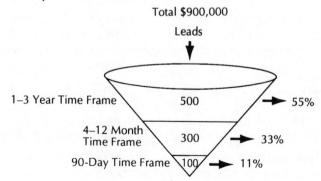

Ellen's pipeline distribution seems reasonable. The problem has to do with volume. Since Ellen's quota is $1 million, she should have $2.5 million in the pipeline, but she has only $900,000 worth of potential business. She will have to take steps to bolster that figure.

5. *Determine the geographic distribution of sales activity.* Now you determine the geographic pockets of the territory that have the highest concentration of prospective business, based on information supplied by a commercial database. Compare this information to Ellen's account activity, with the help of a mapping software program, to determine whether Ellen is concentrating her selling in the areas of highest market potential.

6. *Analyze the distribution of type of activity.* It's a good idea to have underperforming salespeople divide their activities into three areas: administrative (preparing quotes and letters, getting marketing approval for current sales situations, etc.), development of existing accounts, and new account development. Tracking the time they spend in each activity will help poor performing reps to allocate their time more effectively. According to Ellen's daily planner, she is spending her time as follows:

	Percentage of Time
Current account development	72%
Administrative	23
New account development	5

It's clear from the above figures that Ellen is spending far too little time in territory development.

7. *Get agreement and take action.* Once you pinpoint the problems, it's important to get the salesperson's agreement to address and correct them. Here is a summary of what Ellen needs to do in order to improve her time and territory management and bolster sales:

- Spend more time developing the government sector.
- Devote more time to the replacement segment of the electronics market.
- Build the pipeline from its current level ($900,000) to $2.5

million (2.5 × Ellen's quota) by boosting the percentage of time spent developing new accounts from 5 percent to 25 percent.

It may seem like a lot of work to determine the source of a sales problem and work with the salesperson to correct it. But going through this methodical process is more cost-effective and less time-consuming than bringing in a new hire and waiting another three to six months before he or she produces some results. If the salesperson is willing to learn, you should not have to repeat the detailed process above.

Note

1. Part of this discussion is drawn from Joe Petrone, "Reduce Selling Costs (Without Cutting Your Sales Force)," *Personal Selling Power*, January/February 1993: 64.

Chapter 5

Growing in A Competitive Marketplace

With competition intensifying and a growing number of manufacturing operations moving overseas, many U.S. companies in the 1990s are faced with shrinking markets for their products and services. Admonishing reps to "work harder" to make up for a downturn in business in such an environment is unrealistic and demoralizing. The sales manager must work with salespeople to generate more business from current customers and apply creative approaches to locate new customers and market niches.

Profiling Current Customers: The Customer Database

Your current customers are your most valuable source of new business, so it's important to learn all you can about them. One of the most cost effective ways to gather information about customers is by developing a computerized database. This database should contain detailed information about your customers' corporate or personal characteristics, product purchases and applications, markets in which they operate (if they are business customers), and any other information that will help you to target your products and services more effectively.

As markets shrink, the number of competitors courting your customers will increase. You cannot count on your customers' continued loyalty unless you demonstrate that you understand their needs and can satisfy them better than your competitors. A customer database will help you to do so.

Establishing a profile of your customers will give you insight into who buys your products most often and for what uses. This information will aid you in developing and selling additional products to different customer groups.

Once you separate customers into distinct niches, you can target your advertising and sales efforts more closely and develop products more effectively. A database will enable you to measure the success of advertising campaigns and conduct periodic customer surveys to make sure your selling and support efforts are on track. It will also help you to keep current customers updated about new products or product upgrades that are compatible with their current uses. All of these efforts will strengthen your relationship with customers and help to ensure their continued loyalty.

Building a Business-to-Business Customer Database

Following is a summary of the type of information to gather if your customers are other businesses. Depending on your business, you may wish to gather additional data that will help you to address customer needs more effectively.

• *Mailing information.* Include in your database the name, address, phone number, and fax number of each customer, the name and title of the person who purchased the product, and the names and titles of all users.

Knowing the geographic breakdown of customers can help you to uncover buying patterns and preferences that vary by region but might not be obvious without analyzing purchase patterns. This information can help you to target your advertising and selling efforts more carefully.

Update this basic information at least once a year and maybe more, depending on the rate of turnover in your industry. By calling to verify information, you show that you are interested in keeping current with customers, and this will generate additional goodwill. (If John Smith receives a mailer addressed to Mike Jones, who left the position more than a year ago, don't expect him to be receptive to buying from you.)

▪ *Market profile.* It's important to gather information about your customers' markets, so that you will have a better understanding of how your products are used and what product requirements are the most essential to your customers. This information will not only help you to serve customers better today, but it will give you ideas for future products that will closely match customers' unique needs.

For example, universities operate in a far different environment than chemical companies. For one thing, their budgets are far more limited. In purchasing products, they will look for products that require little money to maintain. By understanding the unique characteristics of customers, you will be able to position existing products and develop new ones more effectively.

▪ *Customer industry.* Classify each customer by SIC code to get a picture of the types of businesses that are buying your products or services. These data will tell you what customer groups are of greatest value to the company and will dictate selling strategies. For example, if there is a strong representation of customers in the semiconductor market and a small showing in the food industry, future strategic sales decisions and sales resources can be leveraged toward the former and away from the latter.

▪ *Size of customer company.* Note in your database the size of the customer company, in terms of employees and annual revenues. Knowing the size of company most likely to buy your products will make it possible for your salespeople to focus their selling time. There's not much point in targeting a $5 million company if no such company has ever bought one of your products, because it's too expensive or otherwise inappropriate for this size of firm.

This information will also enable you to develop discount plans for customers that offer the most potential for additional business. For instance, many vendors offer their larger customers graduated discount schedules.

• *Purchase history.* Make sure your database includes an accurate, complete record of every customer purchase, including the purchase date, model number of the product (if applicable), the product configuration, how the product is to be used, and so on. Having the details of purchases will enable you to spot purchase patterns, develop add-on or accessory products, and determine when it's time to approach the customer about replacement products.

The purchase frequency of customers is a good indicator of their potential total value to your firm. Customers whose demand for a particular product is likely to grow faster than your average customer, based on purchase frequency, will be the most profitable and should be targeted for special promotions and discounts.

To ensure that you keep these high-potential customers satisfied, consider surveying them about their postsales expectations, then develop a customer support strategy to meet those expectations. For example, if the customer wants round-the-clock service, figure out how to accommodate that request before one of your competitors does.

• *New product adoption classification.* Classify your customers according to their likelihood of helping you develop and test new products. Companies can be broadly grouped into three categories: innovators, followers, and laggards, depending on their propensity to take risks.

Innovators are risk-takers, those on the cutting edge. Followers are more conservative; they are seldom the first to introduce new products or to buy new ones. They will wait until the innovators have tried and accepted your new product before they will buy it themselves. Laggards tend to stick with the same old products. Their philosophy is "if it ain't broke, don't fix it."

By identifying the innovators among your customer companies and targeting them for new product testing and sales efforts, you will increase your chances of successfully introducing new products. And you will be able to develop appropriate marketing and sales strategies to persuade followers and laggards to buy.

Developing a Retail Customer Database

If you sell to consumers rather than businesses, your database should include mailing information and product purchase history, as described above. It should also include information about customer demographics and "psychographics" (lifestyle), reason for purchase, and information about household buying patterns.

- *Demographics*. By classifying your customer population by age, income, sex, presence of working females, ethnic background, and such, you can determine what product attributes, price, and other criteria appeal to different customer segments.

For example, you may find that high-income people choose your product more than other income groups, or that people who are ages twenty to thirty are more likely to buy your products than those who are thirty-five to forty-five. Rather than design all of your promotional messages for all age and income groups, you can tailor your salespeople's presentations and promotional messages to the appropriate customer niches.

- *Psychographics*. By segmenting your customers according to psychographic or lifestyle data, you can identify differences in buying behavior among different groups of customers. Retired couples are not likely to purchase the same products and services as single working parents. The more you know about your customers' lifestyles, the more effectively you will be able to target products and services to them.

For example, in major urban areas, "meals on wheels" franchises have targeted single working people who have little time to cook or are too tired to visit a restaurant after a long day's work. These franchises offer singles a brochure containing the menus of numerous local restaurants. Customers can order their meals by phone and have them delivered to their homes.

- *Purchase occasion*. Depending on your product, it's good to determine, through a warranty or registration card, whether the product was purchased as a gift or for personal use. If the customer purchased your product as a gift (jewelry, for example), gathering demographic and psychographic information about the buyer may not lead to additional sales.

- *Purchase decision*. Knowing who makes purchase decisions and what their requirements are will also help you to target your selling efforts. For example, if you know that the spouse who makes the decision to purchase furniture is more interested in price than in quality or comfort, you can target mailings about special promotions and clearances to this household.

The best time to start collecting information about potential customers is after they have expressed an interest in your product or service. With current customers, you can update the information in your database by conducting periodic surveys.

Gathering and analyzing customer information via a computerized database can help you to strengthen your relationship with your customers. And developing an accurate profile of current customers can guide you in finding new ones, with the help of external databases, as outlined in Chapter 4.

Finding New Customers: Regional Lead Generation Methods

There is a limit to how many additional products and services you can sell to existing customers. You must continuously search out new customers and markets for your products if your company is to grow and remain competitive.

Traditionally, the marketing department at company headquarters provides leads to the sales department. The lead generation effort from headquarters may involve a variety of activities, such as coordinating seminars, launching direct mail campaigns, and sponsoring trade shows, among other methods.

As companies cut their budgets in response to a tighter economy and shrinking marketplace, the lead generation effort by marketing departments is also being reduced. Regional sales offices will have to pick up the slack.

Even if the corporate budget is healthy, it's still a good idea for the field to take on some of the company's lead generation activities, because some of these activities are done more effectively on a regional than on a national basis. For example, because of disparities in the growth patterns of different regions of the country, a national lead generation system doesn't necessarily benefit all territories. Some economies, such as in the Mountain States and the Midwest, should be growing at a faster rate than others, such as in California and New York, over the next decade. It will require additional work to uncover promising leads in the slower growing areas of the country.

Furthermore, whereas some regions may benefit greatly by advertising in a particular journal, others may see no results from the significant marketing expenditure involved. A particular type of seminar may work better in one territory over another. The same argument holds for other types of lead generation activities aimed at general markets, not specific territories.

A "one-size-fits-all" approach is inadequate to address the unique needs of individual sales regions. It's important to look at each region and territory individually and to develop a customized lead generation program for each one. After leads are gathered from each region, they are then sent to a centralized location at headquarters.

Basic Methods

Following are seven effective methods of lead generation that you can implement in your own region.

1. *Telemarketing.* By having your reps make telephone calls to potential new accounts, you can generate new leads quickly and inexpensively. How much time you dedicate each week to telemarketing and the level of telephone skills of your salespeople will determine the effectiveness of this approach.

If a rep says he is "too busy" to do telemarketing calls, find out why and remove the obstacle. It may be due to a time management problem, or it may be that the rep simply doesn't want to make the calls and uses "lack of time" as an excuse. In that case, you need to work with the rep to help him overcome his fear of the phone. There are excellent telemarketing training courses available for those who are new to the process or need to brush up on their skills.

If time is severely limited and your salespeople's phone skills are poor, you can hire a professional telemarketing firm to make the lead generation calls for you. However, this can add considerably to the expense involved.

Whether you use a professional telemarketing firm or your own reps, this conventional method is and will be one of the fastest and most effective ways to find new customers.

2. *Product seminars.* A product seminar is a cost-effective way to generate new leads and new customers. There are two types

of product seminars: educational seminars for current customers, and seminars directed at prospects for the purpose of generating new leads. Let us discuss the latter.

Prospects do not like to attend seminars in which a manufacturer pitches its products' features. After all, they could read your brochure and get the same information.

The best lead-generating seminars are those that are application-oriented, rather than focused on product features (which prospects can get from your brochure). For example, a technical specialist from your company might discuss how your product has helped different customers to save time and/or money.

To make this lead generation method work, you must schedule a series of seminars at the same location, to build momentum and gain visibility. Ideally, you should hold a seminar each quarter; at a minimum, hold two per year.

If you charge a fee for your seminars, you can cover much of the cost of running them. It doesn't hurt to charge a fee; doing so enhances your image and increases your credibility. People equate "free" with "low quality." A charge of $50 is reasonable and should cover the cost of the room and any food and beverage. If your seminar is well thought out and executed, it should result in substantial word-of-mouth publicity and a number of qualified leads. In one of my sales management positions, our regional office placed an ad for a seminar and received so many qualified responses that we added three more seminars to the schedule.

As more companies jump on the seminar bandwagon, you will have to become more adept at producing and marketing yours. The key to differentiating your seminars from your competitors' will be how well you target your topics to your audiences.

3. *Trade shows*. Trade shows are the mainstay of many companies' lead generation methods. The number of trade shows has more than doubled over the past decade, as competition increases and niches become more specialized. With trade shows proliferating and corporate resources declining, the sales manager must be selective about the choice of shows to attend.

Experience will tell you which of the established trade shows will generate the greatest number of solid leads. For new shows, you can call the show manager and request a registration list. By determining in advance who will be attending the show, you can decide whether or not it is likely to be an effective lead generator.

There are two types of trade shows, horizontal and vertical. Horizontal shows are broad in scope; they include exhibitors from a general market, such as computers. An example of a horizontal show is the COMDEX/Fall annual computer industry show in Las Vegas. One of the largest shows in the United States, it attracts more than 100,000 people and more than 1,700 exhibitors. Usually such shows are sponsored by large exposition companies that plan, organize, and coordinate the events.

Vertical trade shows are more focused. They are attended by customers and exhibitors within a specific segment of a broad market. Often, industry associations sponsor these events. MacWorld is an example of a vertical trade show within a horizontal industry (computers). The show is for users of Macintosh computers and exhibitors who supply peripherals and accessories for the Mac.

In the future, growth will occur mainly in the vertical trade show market, because these present the greatest opportunity for increased sales. With time and resources at a premium, people are more likely to attend only those shows that are closely targeted to their needs and interests. For this reason, vertical trade shows, with their narrow focus, are more likely to generate high-quality leads than are generalized, horizontal shows.

4. *Print advertising.* There are two categories of advertisements, image and lead generation. An image advertisement focuses on a generalized quality of the company. For example, it might emphasize that the company is "number one in customer satisfaction." The primary objective of this type of advertisement is simply to strengthen the company's image in the eyes of customers and prospects.

An ad designed to generate leads will be more focused than an image advertisement. Instead of conveying a generalized quality of the company, it will stress product benefits, or show how a product satisfies a particular customer need better than existing technology or competitors' products. The primary objective is not to boost the company's image but to get prospects to mail a request for product information or pick up the phone and place an order.

To generate additional leads on a tight budget, you can place low-cost advertisements in the publications of local business groups, such as the Chamber of Commerce. Association newsletters also solicit advertisements. For as little as $200, you can place a full-page insert or at least a half-page ad in these newsletters. This is far less expensive than advertising in trade journals or local newspapers, and can be equally effective at reaching your target market.

Be sure to make it easy for readers to respond; a toll-free number is the best. It's good to support the claims you make in the ad by using testimonials of satisfied customers, or by showing your guarantee. Another way to increase response is to offer the reader a free gift for replying. Make sure that your ad stresses what the reader will gain by using your product.

5. *Customer and prospect referrals.* Customers can be a fertile source of referrals. The majority of customers, if they are satisfied with your product and/or service, will be happy to give you referrals, if only you ask. But in my experience, few salespeople bother to ask customers for leads.

In some cases, even prospects who don't buy your product or service can be a good source of referrals. As long as you've shown a sincere interest in the prospect and made a legitimate attempt to satisfy his or her needs, you are justified in asking for referrals. If you have handled yourself well in the selling process, you can expect to get a positive response, even if the prospect is not interested in buying from you.

6. *Lead network groups.* Networking is another good way of generating sales leads. One of the most effective variations is to network with salespeople from other companies in a variety of industries.

In most major urban areas, you can find lead network groups that provide a structured format for generating leads. These groups, which are usually sponsored by the Chamber of Commerce or other local business organizations, generally meet once a week and may include as many as forty or more people. Attendance is limited to one salesperson or business owner per product type. For example, you won't find two reps selling office furniture in the same lead network group.

Here's how it works: Each person goes around the room and tells every member of the group about his or her most recent client. The members, in turn, ask questions to determine whether the client described might need their products or services as well. For example, when a commercial real estate salesperson mentions a new client, an office furniture salesperson might inquire whether the client needs new office furniture.

You don't have to belong to a lead network group in order to generate leads through other salespeople. For example, Emily, who sells real estate services, sets up a breakfast meeting with a salesperson from a different (noncompeting) company every month for the purpose of generating new leads. Emily has used this approach with great success, in large part because she makes a point of trying to help the other person before she asks for information that might help her.

The first thing she says to every new person who joins her for breakfast is: "Please tell me enough about your business and your products so that I'll know when I see a potential customer I can send to you."

Emily also sends a thank you note to every person she meets this way. Because she shows a genuine interest in helping others, they are eager to help her by supplying any leads they can. Even if they don't have any leads when they meet with Emily, she is no doubt one of the first people they think of when they come across someone who needs the real estate services she provides.

Despite its potential, networking with other salespeople is one of the least used methods of lead generation. I have seen very few salespeople master the process of getting leads through other salespeople. One of the most common reasons is that they fail to consider the needs of the other person, as Emily does.

Don't expect to get until you give. Before you ask someone for a referral, demonstrate an interest in satisfying his or her needs.

Networking is one of the slower lead generation strategies. But because it's based on relationship building, it can lead to a steady stream of new contacts, making it one of the most success-ful methods in the long run. It is also one of the least costly ways of finding new customers.

7. *Direct mail advertising.* Direct mail advertising is a widely used (and in my experience, highly effective) method of generat-ing new leads. It can involve anything from a simple one-page flyer to a customized letter to an elaborate wooden box with a

prop inside that is intended to get the recipient to take action, such as calling a toll-free number for product information.

If done properly, direct mail can reduce your advertising costs (without reducing advertising effectiveness) by enabling you to target only those prospects who are the most likely to buy your products.

To generate the highest response rate possible, you must develop an effective ad, select the most appropriate mailing lists, and do repeat mailings.

To develop an effective direct mail advertisement, enlist the support of someone from your marketing department to help you with design and layout. Or, consult one of the numerous books on the subject of direct mail. The Direct Marketing Association, headquartered in New York City, can refer you to some excellent sources of information. If you can afford it, you might consider hiring a direct mail expert to help you develop the first few advertisements and to teach you how to develop your own ads in the future.

Once you've developed your ad, you must send it to the right people. Your mailing lists will come from one or more of three sources: your own database of prospects and customers, a list compiler or broker (discussed in Chapter 4), and trade journals, which will rent you lists of people who have responded to specific advertisements placed in their publications.

To make direct mail work, you must send several pieces over a relatively short period of time. Repetition reinforces your message, helps people to remember your name, and makes it more likely that they will purchase your product, or at least inquire about it.

Before you do a massive mailing, test two or three versions of your direct mail piece to see which one generates the highest response rate. Suppose you want to do a mailing to 10,000 customers or prospects. Send a different version of the mailer to three groups of 1,000 each and see which version "pulls" the best. Send that version to the remaining 7,000 people on your list.

Once you get a response, follow it up with a telephone call. If you are mailing to a limited number of business customers, call every customer after you've done the mailing; this will ensure a higher response rate.

Successful companies pursue many or all of the lead generation activities outlined above, and they execute them well. The key word is "execute." A poorly run trade show, badly managed seminar, or ineffective direct mail campaign can hurt rather than help your business. Whatever approaches you choose, make sure you give them your best effort.

No single approach is necessarily better than any other. Whether or not a given approach will generate a significant number of leads depends on the nature of the product or service you're selling, the type of customer, and the region of the country you're targeting, among other factors. By understanding in detail how your customers do business and by testing various approaches, you will be able to determine which approaches are most effective for you.

Once your lead generation program is underway, you can check to see which activities are producing the greatest number of high quality leads. One simple method is to keep track of how new customers learned about your company. I tracked this for twelve months in one of my sales management jobs and generated a graph, shown in Figure 5-1. With this information, I could determine the gap between the number of leads generated by the national lead program and the number needed to meet our regional quota.

As Figure 5-1 indicates, the national lead generation program produced $7.1 million in sales during the year the information was tracked. To reach our regional goal of $8 million, we needed to generate additional leads. We focused on areas such as direct

Figure 5-1. Results of national lead generation program.

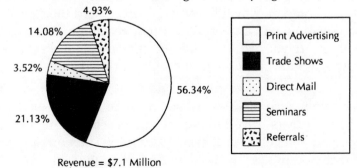

mail that we felt were promising but had not been effective when done by corporate headquarters because they were not tightly targeted.

Innovative Methods of Lead Generation

Once you have mastered the basic lead generation methods outlined above, start looking at new and innovative ways of getting new leads. As competition increases and markets become saturated, your customers and prospects will be inundated with direct mail ads and bombarded with sales pitches. As a result, you will have to find more and more creative ways to generate leads if you want to give your company an edge over the competition. Following are four innovative sources of leads:

1. *Specialty trade shows.* Rather than attending trade shows run by exposition companies, consider sponsoring your own one- to two-day "specialty" trade show. This gives you maximum control over the theme of the show, the types of exhibitors who will participate, and the people who will attend.

First, determine which group of customers and/or prospects you wish to invite. Next, develop a theme that will attract them to the show. (For example, a computer company might put on a show with the theme of how to protect computer systems from theft and viruses.) Then, identify noncompeting companies that fit in with your theme and who are willing to help you plan and organize the event. In addition to having exhibits, present application-based papers related to the theme of your show.

It's important to team up with companies who are leaders in their field and who are known for innovation. Your association with these companies will boost your image, and their participation in the show will attract more attendees and a higher caliber of attendee. If you do your job effectively, your show should generate a significant number of highly qualified leads.

2. *Customer-led seminars.* In addition to holding seminars given by your technical specialists, arrange a series of talks by selected customers. If you invite prestigious clients to be seminar leaders, you will generate curiosity and interest among prospects for your company's products or services. And you will strengthen

your relationship with the customers who participate in the seminars.

I have seen this approach work with great success among user groups of personal computers and software products. At these seminars, users tell how they are applying the products and describe the benefits of using them. Because it is the buyer rather than the seller who is praising the product, the message carries more credibility and is likely to generate more leads.

I once started a user group among buyers of our company's scientific products. We started with fifteen people, all of them customers. I regularly sought their input about future meetings. The best advice I received was to expand the range of product topics.

This not only gave the existing group more to discuss among themselves, but it generated a lot of word-of-mouth advertising and attracted a new and diverse group of members, including many excellent prospects as well as customers. Over the next year, our user group grew from fifteen people to more than seventy regular attendees.

3. *Formal agreements to trade leads.* Earlier I encouraged you to network with other salespeople in order to generate new leads. You can take this one step further by setting up a formal agreement with salespeople from noncompeting companies within the same broad market (e.g., health care or computers). The objective is the same as for networking: to generate leads from other companies who are selling complementary products or services.

After you identify these companies, ask their sales managers to meet with you and draft a formal agreement whereby the salespeople of each company pass along leads to the appropriate reps in other companies. A fee is paid by the company who gets the lead, if it results in an order being booked. The fee can vary from 1 percent to 10 percent of the order.

I know of one financial services company that participates in such an arrangement. The company finances the accounts receivable of cash-hungry businesses. It passes along the names of new customers to a data processing firm, which takes on labor-intensive payroll and data processing projects for cash-strapped companies, so they can minimize payroll expenses and maximize flexibility. The data processing firm, in turn, passes along the names of cash-strapped businesses that the financial services company might be able to help. It's a winning situation for both companies and for customers, who receive information about valuable services they might otherwise have overlooked.

4. *On-line computer conferences.* Consumers are using on-line computer services to purchase clothing, electronic, and other goods without leaving their homes. All that's required is a personal computer with a modem installed. With a modem, a host telephone number, and a password, they can access a variety of on-line catalogs of retail goods.

As on-line computer services become more affordable and computers more widely used, more consumers will subscribe. In addition to purchasing goods and making product inquiries through on-line computer services, people will increasingly use them to get additional product information from companies and to exchange tips with other users, either one-on-one or via electronic user conferences.

If your company subscribes to one of these on-line services, such as CompuServe, you can use it to communicate with customers and prospects and to generate new leads. For example, you can offer new product information or product updates through the service, answer queries electronically, and organize on-line user conferences to discuss specific applications topics. You can also install a library of informational papers that users can access at their computers. If you provide relevant, useful, timely information through an on-line computer service, you will generate many high-quality leads, on an ongoing basis, through word of mouth.

Additional Growth Strategies

In addition to tracking your customers' needs via a computerized database and actively generating new leads, there are several other ways you can ensure that your company maintains a competitive edge. One of the best ways is to recruit high-quality salespeople.

Recruit and Retain Top Salespeople

If you make a concerted effort to hire top salespeople and offer them ample rewards and recognition, you will be in a better position to retain current customers and find new ones. Hiring top salespeople is no small task. High performers are usually well respected and well paid in their current companies, so luring them away is a challenge.

One way to recruit new talent is to participate in career expos and job fairs. For $1,000 to $4,000, you can set up a booth at a major expo or fair and talk with prospective job candidates. This is an excellent way to fill an empty pipeline with potential recruits.

Another method is to set up a relationship with two or three executive recruiters, before you need to fill a position. Tell them you do not have any openings now, but that you would like them to present you with potential candidates to interview once a quarter. Let them know you are talking to other recruiters, but that they will have first shot at filling an opening if the candidates they send are the most qualified.

This approach produces two powerful results. You are made aware of available talent on a regular basis, and you educate recruiters on your selection criteria for new hires.

Once you've hired the best, you must make every effort to retain them. In my experience, the most successful salespeople are those who have been in their territories for more than three years. That's because in my industry, the cycle from interest to purchase can be years long. The prospect who starts a conversation with a salesperson in 1988 may not purchase a product until 1991.

Even if your sales cycle is shorter—say, a year or less—customers and prospects will feel more comfortable if they know your company's sales force is stable. To outsiders, stability in sales representation means that the company is solid and that support will be available after the sale.

There is a negative side to the long-tenured salesperson. People who have been in sales for many years may reach a plateau. They may know their customers and territories so well that they tend to coast rather than make things happen.

To keep veteran salespeople motivated, give them extra responsibilities. For example, I once took a veteran top producer whose enthusiasm was waning and asked him to train a new hire. The veteran got the benefit of a fresh experience and felt more involved with the company because he was responsible for the growth and development of a newcomer. And this experience made him an even more valuable contributor to the company's ongoing success.

Besides providing challenging responsibilities, offer an attractive compensation package. If you offer a competitive salary and commission structure, your top performers are not as likely to be wooed away by competitors.

Train and Develop Your Sales Force

Another way to retain top performers is to offer ongoing training and development. No matter how skilled a salesperson may be, there is always room for improvement in some area. Work with your salespeople to identify areas that they feel need improvement. Once you've jointly identified areas in which training might help, send the reps to appropriate training courses, then follow up with hands-on coaching to make sure they apply what they've learned.

If your budget is limited, conduct some of the training yourself. I once had a salesperson named Martha who needed training in telephone prospecting. Rather than telling Martha how to prospect on the phone, I wrote down all the steps involved, then made a call myself, so that she could observe how it was done.

Then I asked Martha to try. For the next hour, we took turns making calls. At first she was nervous, but after a few calls the nervousness subsided and her technique improved significantly. After we finished the calls, I showed her how to measure her effectiveness, by using a chart to track the number of calls made and completed and the "hit rate" for each telephone session.

Figure 5-2 shows Martha's chart. Martha learned how many calls must be attempted to receive an acceptable number of leads.

Figure 5-2. Telephone lead effectiveness report.

Date	Day	Attempted Calls	Completed Calls	Leads	Hit Rate	Length of Time
7/16/93	Friday	30	8	3	0.375	60 mins.
7/29/93	Thursday	26	6	2	0.33	50 mins.
8/03/93	Wednesday	15	3	1	0.33	30 mins.

Too often, salespeople attempt fifteen calls and give up after only one lead. By using the lead effectiveness report, they can measure how much effort is required to generate leads. The "day" field is included to track which day is best to contact a given type of client. With some solid training and a measurement tool—the telephone lead effectiveness report—in hand, Martha soon became comfortable and proficient in telephone prospecting.

By offering ongoing training, you ensure that your sales force will have an edge over the competitor's.

Improve the Overall Won/Lost Ratio

Another way to grow your business in a competitive market is by striving to improve the overall won/lost ratio of your sales force. In one company I worked for, salespeople were expected to produce a won/lost ratio of at least 50 percent. This high ratio reflected the number of orders reps needed to win in order for the company to retain its leadership position in the market.

Knowing your salespeople need to achieve a high won/lost ratio is only the beginning. If the current ratio is 20 percent and you want to boost it to 50 percent, you must look for the source of the 30 percent gap. You may need to go on a few sales calls with the salesperson in order to identify the problem. Perhaps the rep needs more product knowledge, or additional training in a particular skill area. Once you determine the problem, you can work one-on-one with the rep to create a strategy for solving it.

Uncover Hidden Sales Situations

Once your reps have achieved a high won/lost ratio, capturing additional market share requires that they uncover new sales situations in which to participate. Specifically, your salespeople need to find out about those potential customers who contact the competition rather than your company when they're ready to buy a product. These hidden sales situations represent an untapped source of potential business and the opportunity to win market share from competitors.

A good starting point is to identify your competitors' key accounts. You can get this information by looking first at your own database and determining which customers have the potential to buy multiple products. If they aren't approaching your company about buying, they are no doubt calling on your competitors.

You can also make use of an external database, as described in Chapter 4, to identify all of the companies in your territory or region who are potential customers. Based on the total market potential and average selling price of your products or services, you can approximate the total number of selling situations occurring each quarter in a given territory.

Based on experience, it's reasonable to expect that a salesperson will be aware of, and participate in, 70 percent of the total sales situations in his or her territory. You can determine whether or not they are doing so by adding the number of orders won and lost, as recorded in the Won/Lost report your reps fill out each month. They should add up to at least 70 percent of the total market figure.

For example, if there are ten total sales situations in the territory this quarter, your rep should be participating in seven of them. To win market share from competitors, the rep must find and actively solicit the remaining three prospects and woo them away from the competition. One way to do this is by adopting a customer-focused selling strategy (discussed in detail in Chapter 7).

Develop a Customer Focused-Based Sales Strategy For Low-End Products

If your company sells commodity products that are not easily differentiated from those of your competitors, switching the focus of your sales pitch can help you to win market share. In computers and many other technology-oriented markets, product prices are falling and performance is increasing. The low end is the fastest growing segment of many high tech and other commodity markets. Many companies that formerly focused on the high end of these markets are now entering the low end, which holds the greatest potential for increasing market share.

To be successful in this price-sensitive market segment, salespeople must position their products differently than if they were selling high-end products. The requirements and technological sophistication of the buyer of a $100,000 piece of technology are different than those of the purchaser of a $5,000 system. Specifically, buyers in the low end of technology markets are more cost-conscious and less technologically savvy than those in the high end. Sales strategies must be adjusted accordingly.

Selling a $100,000 system to a PhD in a major university requires that the sales rep schedule elaborate technical demonstrations and bring in technical people to talk about product details. Usually, these buyers know exactly what they want in the way of technical specifications, since they had to supply extensive documentation in order to receive funding for the equipment. Their ultimate buying decision will be based on the technical superiority of one product over another.

Selling a $10,000 or less system is a far different experience. At this product level, buyers are generally more interested in whether or not you can beat your competitor's price than in all of the technical features of your product.

Buyers at this level generally don't have the time or knowledge to understand the technical differences among products. They may have trouble comparing products even if they try, since different companies may use different terminology to describe the same product features.

All of which means that your salespeople must sell these buyers using a customer-focused sales strategy. This is especially important if your product is not the lowest priced in the market. In that case, a competitor can claim that your higher priced product is no better than their less expensive one, based on features. Even if this is not true, the buyer may not know any better.

Instead of comparing the price and features of your company's product to the lower priced models of competitors, your salespeople should stress the superior advantages of your higher priced product related to your customer's needs. In this way, prospects will understand that your product has a greater value that justifies the higher price. And they will more likely be impressed by your customer-oriented approach than by the approach of a competitor who stresses only low price and features.

Implementing the strategies presented in this chapter requires a serious commitment, but one that is well worth the effort involved. By keeping current customers satisfied, using creative approaches to win new business, hiring, training, and developing a topnotch sales force, and consistently practicing the other techniques outlined above, you can stay one step ahead no matter how competitive your marketplace becomes.

Perhaps the most powerful strategy for winning and retaining customers is to offer a high level of quality and service. That's the focus of the next two chapters.

Chapter 6
Total Quality Selling

Total Quality Management (TQM) continues to be a major focus of American business. However, much of the focus has been on manufacturing; little emphasis has been placed on quality in the sales organization. A study by Learning International found that less than 10 percent of companies have incorporated the concept of quality into the daily activities of their sales forces. If only one out of ten companies focuses on quality in the area of sales, your company can gain a significant advantage over its competitors by implementing a Total Quality Selling strategy.

Why is it important for the sales department to focus on quality? Because the customer's first contact with a company is often through a salesperson. Customers form an opinion about the quality of an organization based on how the salesperson treats them. It doesn't matter how high quality a company's products are if customers decide not to buy them because they've been treated poorly by the people who sell them.

Despite the importance of implementing quality in the sales organization, it's not surprising that quality improvement programs have largely been confined to manufacturing. After all, manufacturing is a repetitive, controllable process that focuses on tangible products and is thus easy to measure, control, and improve.

By contrast, sales is a variable process that focuses on intangible relationships. There is no easy definition of sales quality and no objective measures of it. And the sales process is more difficult to control because it is variable and because it occurs, not under a single roof, but in the offices of customers scattered throughout a territory or region. These are just a few of the reasons why sales organizations have failed to implement quality procedures.

However, if we look at quality in a different light, the similarities between manufacturing and sales quality can be seen, and the obstacles to implementing quality in the sales organization can be overcome. If we reduce quality to its most basic definition, it is the same for sales as it is for manufacturing: quality is simply *meeting and exceeding customer expectations*.

In the case of manufacturing, customers may expect products to have certain features and to be free of defects. In the case of sales, customers may expect the salesperson to listen to their needs, to treat them with courtesy, to give them the information they need to make the purchase decision, and not to pressure them into buying. In either case, the level of quality is determined by the extent to which the customer's expectations are met.

It is the *customer's* perception, not the company's, that should drive quality efforts. There is often a gap between the customer's and the company's perception of quality. For example, a company might perceive that its two-week response time to customer orders is more than satisfactory. But if the customer expects a one-week delivery, the company has failed to meet the buyer's expectations. The focus of all quality efforts must be on bridging the gap between customer perceptions of quality and company performance.

Trust and Empathy: Keys to Quality in Sales

Customers judge the quality of a product by assessing its "hard" dimensions, such as product features, performance, reliability, durability, ease of use, and price. To judge the quality of a salesperson, they look for the "soft" factors such as trust and empathy. These "soft" dimensions are critical in selling, especially in companies that offer commodity products. When customers cannot tell the difference between one product and another, they will likely buy from the salesperson they trust the most, the one who demonstrates the "soft" qualities of caring, respect, and, most of all, empathy.

Unfortunately, these soft dimensions—which are the salesperson's most powerful asset—are often ignored or minimized, because they are difficult to measure and because salespeople receive product training, not training in empathy.

Salespeople are generally effective at talking about product specifications, performance data, and other hard dimensions, which are easy to measure. They are often less effective at building trust by showing empathy for the customer's needs.

Trust is the essential ingredient in quality selling. At the end of a selling process that is built on trust, the customer has no lingering concerns or doubts because he or she has expressed them to the sales rep and has been satisfied with the rep's responses.

Not every salesperson gains the trust of the customer. Think about the last time you made a substantial purchase. If you shopped around, there may have been three or four salespeople telling you how great their product is. Did you express your innermost concerns to each salesperson, or to the person you trusted the most? Why did you trust him or her? If you think back, you will probably find that it's because the person showed a genuine interest in meeting your needs rather than merely making the sale. In other words, the salesperson showed empathy.

Empathy is simply another word for understanding. It involves more than asking the customer a set of canned questions about product uses and the features the customer desires. It's about listening to customers' needs, understanding their concerns, putting oneself into the customer's shoes. Chapter 7 explores the differences between the sales-driven salesperson, who is only interested in getting the order, and the customer-focused salesperson, whose main goal is to satisfy the customer, not close the sale. A central difference between these two types of salespeople is the quality of empathy.

Perhaps it's easiest to describe empathy by giving an example involving a seven-month effort by Guy, a financial services representative. During this period, Guy developed a proposal to save a consumer products firm more than $100,000 over a five-year period by switching to an alternative carrier of business insurance. The chief financial officer of the firm was ready to accept the proposal, but when he approached the executive council, not all of the members shared his enthusiasm over Guy's recommendation.

Guy, who was anxious to collect his $10,000 commission on the proposal, began to receive polite stalling tactics from the CFO. Rather than trying to force a sale, Guy worked with the CFO in an attempt to understand the true cause of the council members' reluctance.

After answering all of the CFO's technical concerns, it became obvious that the issue had nothing to do with the product Guy was offering. Rather, it was the sales rep's hunch that two of the members of the executive council were loyal to the current carrier and didn't want to make a switch. His hunch was based on the tone of voice and defensive comments made on behalf of the current carrier.

Instead of trying to force the issue, Guy told the CFO and the two executive council members: "If loyalty is the issue, I cannot continue to take up your time, because I respect the value of loyalty in a business relationship."

This demonstration of unselfish empathy made the executives realize that a decision must be made between loyalty and saving money. And it helped the council members to make a more objective decision, rather than a purely emotional one. They decided they could not pass up the $100,000 savings that Guy's proposal represented. They switched carriers, thanks to the low pressure and high empathy level of this financial sales representative.

Continuous Improvement

Whether in manufacturing or sales, quality is achieved and sustained by monitoring and controlling the process every step of the way, by making small, continuous improvements, what the Japanese refer to as *kaizen*. Quality gurus such as W. Edwards Demings, Joseph Juran, and Phil Crosby stress different techniques for achieving quality. But they all subscribe to the concept of continuous improvement, of moving toward Total Quality by focusing on quality (i.e., on meeting and exceeding customer expectations) in every aspect of the job.

Continuous improvement is achieved by focusing on the

customer on a continuous basis, by monitoring salespeople and giving them frequent feedback, through process improvement tools, such as training and progressive goal management and such quality-building tools as the Pareto chart (discussed in Chapter 8), and by rewarding salespeople for their efforts toward achieving total quality.

Customer Focus

One way to achieve continuous improvement in sales is by constantly focusing on customers. Among other things, this involves maintaining the relationship with the customer after the sale, monitoring their needs on a regular basis, soliciting their input (and using it), and showing appreciation for their business.

One simple way to demonstrate a customer focus is by making it easy for customers to communicate with you, by installing a toll-free number for your sales and support functions. An 800 number gives the customer an added incentive to talk with your sales office. And it prevents customers who require support from feeling resentful that they must pay for the phone call.

To maintain the relationship with the customer after the sale, send periodic newsletters or application notes that let customers know about new products and product enhancements. These newsletters should be accompanied by a brief note from the salesperson, such as "Jill, let me know how the new product is working. Here are some enhancements that might interest you." If your company offers customer training, let customers know about that as well.

Hold customer focus groups on a regular basis to stay in touch with changing customer expectations and to allow customers to express their concerns or discuss product problems.

As companies become "leaner and meaner," they are looking for ways to identify new market opportunities with fewer marketing people. One way is to rely more on salespeople for product development suggestions. Customers are the single best source of new product ideas, and soliciting customers' input is another way of maintaining close relationships with them.

Get customers involved in the product development process by holding brainstorming meetings to generate new product

ideas and ideas for product enhancements. Surveys and interviews are other effective means of generating new product ideas
from customers. Having these meetings regularly will ensure that
your sales and marketing efforts are in sync with customers'
needs.

To spark the enthusiasm of the sales force about soliciting
new product ideas from customers, hold a contest. During a
specified period of time, encourage salespeople to give their ideas
for new products or product enhancements to a designated
person in marketing. Have a panel review the ideas and select
those that will contribute the most to the new product planning
process. Give the salespeople who come up with the top three
ideas a cash award. (Make sure it's substantial enough to provide
a real incentive.)

Such contests are valuable for the marketing department,
because they may reveal patterns in the thinking of customers
that can guide the product development effort. For example, if a
number of reps come up with ideas for automating various
products, automation may be a key concern of customers, and
adding automation capabilities to your products may give you a
competitive advantage.

Let your customers know how much you appreciate their
business by hosting an annual party in their honor. Bring your
company's top sales, marketing, and engineering managers to
this party to bring the customer in closer contact with the executive suite. These meetings bridge the gap between upper management's perception and the customer's reality.

To help your field salespeople to maintain their customer
focus, send them articles on quality, testimonials from satisfied
customers, and examples of customer-focused goals developed
by salespeople throughout the company. The point is to remind
them continuously that meeting customer's needs is their number
one goal.

Measurement and Feedback

Measurement is critical to achieving continuous sales improvement. But when implementing quality programs, some companies get carried away with measurements and lose sight of their
purpose. You must be careful to measure only those things that

relate to your goal of meeting and exceeding customer expectations.

Before instituting any sales quality measurement, ask yourself: Will measuring this behavior or activity help the salesperson to serve the customer better? If the answer is no, there is no need to measure it. That includes some commonly measured activities such as the number of sales calls a rep makes. Better to measure the number of repeat orders generated, which can be related to customer satisfaction.

One salesperson of a bearing manufacturer was bragging to me about his company's TQM program. I asked him if quality was implemented in the sales organization. Proudly, he recited the different ways that sales quality was measured.

As he kept talking, I tried to look for the connection between his sales department's quality efforts and customer satisfaction, but I could find none. Most of the "quality" efforts he mentioned had to do with measuring activities, such as the number of sales calls made in a quarter. They had nothing to do with meeting customer expectations or achieving high levels of customer satisfaction.

Following are some valid ways of measuring customer satisfaction.

▪ *Conducting customer surveys.* What *should* be measured are gaps between your customers' expectations and your salespeople's performance. One way to discover gaps is by surveying customers to find out how well your salespeople are meeting their current expectations and to learn of any new expectations.

A brief mail or telephone survey should be implemented immediately after an order has been placed or business has been lost. Only by finding out what you are doing right and wrong can you improve the selling process.

There are pros and cons to surveying by telephone and mail. With the telephone, you can generate faster responses than you could by mail. Telephone surveys are more expensive than mail surveys, but the response rate is generally higher. However, you can't go into as much detail by phone as you can by mail. A sample mail survey is shown in Figure 6-1.

After collecting and tabulating the data from the surveys,

(Text continues on page 120)

Figure 6-1. Sample customer survey.

ABC Company Field Sales Survey

Please take a moment to complete this survey. Your responses will improve our sales force's ability to exceed our customers' expectations.

1. Presents technical information *clearly.*

Importance	Very Important		Uncertain		Not Important
of this factor to you	1	2	3	4	5
Satisfaction	Strongly Agree		Uncertain		Strongly Disagree
of this factor to you	1	2	3	4	5

2. Explains *only* those product features that benefit us.

Importance	Very Important		Uncertain		Not Important
of this factor to you	1	2	3	4	5
Satisfaction	Strongly Agree		Uncertain		Strongly Disagree
of this factor to you	1	2	3	4	5

3. Shows how relevant product features *differ* from the competition.

Importance	Very Important		Uncertain		Not Important
of this factor to you	1	2	3	4	5
Satisfaction	Strongly Agree		Uncertain		Strongly Disagree
of this factor to you	1	2	3	4	5

4. Shows good *understanding* of products.

Importance	Very Important		Uncertain		Not Important
of this factor to you	1	2	3	4	5
Satisfaction	Strongly Agree		Uncertain		Strongly Disagree
of this factor to you	1	2	3	4	5

5. Acts as a *consultant* (looks at both sides) in trying to get his or her point
   accepted.

Importance	Very Important		Uncertain		Not Important
of this factor to you	1	2	3	4	5
Satisfaction	Strongly Agree		Uncertain		Strongly Disagree
of this factor to you	1	2	3	4	5

6. Shows understanding of *our* point of view.

Importance	Very Important		Uncertain		Not Important
of this factor to you	1	2	3	4	5
Satisfaction	Strongly Agree		Uncertain		Strongly Disagree
of this factor to you	1	2	3	4	5

7. Helps *analyze* our needs through intelligent questions.

Importance	Very Important		Uncertain		Not Important
of this factor to you	1	2	3	4	5
Satisfaction	Strongly Agree		Uncertain		Strongly Disagree
of this factor to you	1	2	3	4	5

Figure 6-1. Sample customer survey *(continued)*.

8. Is *pleasing* to deal with.

Importance	Very Important		Uncertain		Not Important
of this factor to you	1	2	3	4	5
Satisfaction	Strongly Agree		Uncertain		Strongly Disagree
of this factor to you	1	2	3	4	5

9. Develops working relationships *easily*.

Importance	Very Important		Uncertain		Not Important
of this factor to you	1	2	3	4	5
Satisfaction	Strongly Agree		Uncertain		Strongly Disagree
of this factor to you	1	2	3	4	5

10. Shows genuine interest in knowing special requirements of *our business*.

Importance	Very Important		Uncertain		Not Important
of this factor to you	1	2	3	4	5
Satisfaction	Strongly Agree		Uncertain		Strongly Disagree
of this factor to you	1	2	3	4	5

11. Resolves our concerns by being a good *listener*.

Importance	Very Important		Uncertain		Not Important
of this factor to you	1	2	3	4	5
Satisfaction	Strongly Agree		Uncertain		Strongly Disagree
of this factor to you	1	2	3	4	5

12. Asks for decisions *without* being aggressive.

Importance	Very Important		Uncertain		Not Important
of this factor to you	1	2	3	4	5
Satisfaction	Strongly Agree		Uncertain		Strongly Disagree
of this factor to you	1	2	3	4	5

13. What is your occupation? _____

14. _____ Check if you would like someone from ABC Company to contact you about this survey.

15. How can we improve the quality of ABC Company field sales?

_____

_____

_____

_____

Thank you!

post the results for each salesperson in the form of a Pareto chart (Figure 6-2). This type of chart gives salespeople a clear picture of their strengths and the areas that need improvement.

Figure 6-2 was constructed out of the data from the survey shown in Figure 6-1. The chart shows how the salesperson scored in the following areas:

Developing rapport (Questions 8–10)
Analyzing needs (Question 7)
Showing empathy (Questions 5 and 6)
Resolving concerns (Question 11)
Presentation (Questions 1–4)
Closing (Question 12)

The height of the bars is determined by calculating the number of responses with a value of 4 or 5 in any given category. For example, in Figure 6-2, the salesperson received eight scores of 4 or 5 in the category of analyzing needs (Question 7), signaling that this is an area where the salesperson needs improvement. Once you have identified areas that require improvement, based on customers' responses, make sure you provide your salespeople with the training they need to overcome their deficiencies.

It's a good idea to conduct these customer surveys every three months and to construct Pareto charts on a quarterly basis, so that you can monitor your reps' progress and so they can literally see where they are improving or falling short. It's also important to recognize and reward those salespeople who show the most improvement.

Initially you may see some defensive behavior as you use the Pareto diagram. Explain that the diagrams are not meant to be used to punish people. Rather, they are simply another form of feedback, from the most important source: the customer.

TAKING CONCRETE ACTION TO MEET CUSTOMER NEEDS: GRANITE ROCK

Granite Rock Company is a $90-million firm based in Watsonville, California. It produces rock, sand, and gravel aggregates,

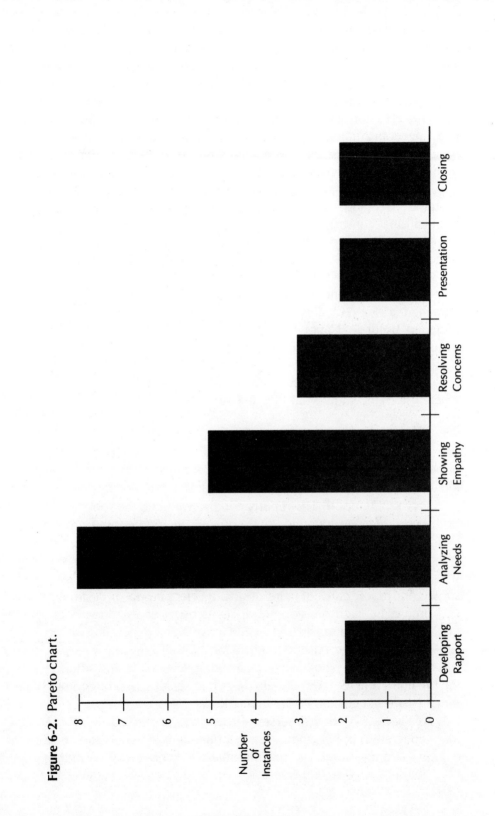

Figure 6-2. Pareto chart.

ready-mix concrete, asphalt, road treatments, and recycled road-base material for sale to commercial and residential builders and highway construction companies. The company, which employs roughly 400 workers, also retails building materials made by other manufacturers and runs a highway paving operation.

Granite Rock operates in a competitive marketplace in which customers demand high quality and most competitors are owned by multinational construction material companies with deep pockets.

Because the products Granite Rock sells are commodities, it's difficult to differentiate one supplier from another. One factor that separates Granite Rock from its tough competition is quality.

Granite Rock knows a lot about quality. The company, which launched a Total Quality Program in 1985, won the prestigious Malcolm Baldrige National Quality Award in 1992, thanks to its strong focus on meeting and exceeding customer needs.

A primary reason Granite Rock is so successful at meeting customer needs is that the company takes great pains to find out what customers want, what they like about Granite Rock, and what needs improving.

Each time customers do business with Granite Rock, the company asks them to fill out "quick response" cards that give them the opportunity to "comment on the service and products you received today." Every customer complaint generates a product-service discrepancy (PSD) report. The reports are reviewed and the root causes of the problems are identified and corrected. Periodic focus groups let the company probe for ideas about new products and services.

At the core of Granite Rock's quality efforts are customer surveys. Every year since 1987, Granite Rock divisions have mailed a survey or "report card" (Figure 6-3) to a select group of customers and prospects. Each division conducts its own survey. Surveys are mailed to anywhere from 100 to 1,500 customers, depending on the size of the customer base at each plant. Not all customers receive surveys, only those who have done a certain level of business during the previous year. Surveys are also sent to a select group of contractors who are not customers of Granite Rock.

As Figure 6-3 shows, survey respondents are asked to list the three concrete suppliers they use most often and to assign each one a grade, from A to F, in several quality-related areas including

Figure 6-3. Granite Rock: annual "report card."

salespeople. Granite Rock uses this information as a benchmark to compare itself to the competition and pinpoint areas that need improvement. A grade of C means that a given company is the same as the competition in that area.

Afterward, a Quality Team reviews the survey results and decides on the actions to take. When a survey comes back and Granite Rock is not listed as one of the three most-used suppliers, the company uses the information to make quality improvements. Greg Diehl, marketing services manager, notes: "That is a really important piece of marketing intelligence. . . . They are telling us what we need to do to get them as a customer."

The survey helps Granite Rock's sales team make calls on customers. Salespeople never use the results of the "report card" to make comparisons between Granite Rock and the competition during sales call, but the sales staff is made aware of what is most important to customers.

In addition to sending out an annual report card, at least once every three years (usually every other year) Granite Rock asks ready-mix customers to rank the importance of several influences in buying concrete (Figure 6-4), including:

Figure 6-4. Granite Rock: importance survey.

What Is Important to *YOU?*

Please rate each of the following on a scale from 1 to 5 with 5 being most important in your decision to purchase from a supplier.

	Importance	Concrete Least . . . Most	Building Materials Least . . . Most
Responsive to special needs		1 2 3 4 5	1 2 3 4 5
Easy to place orders		1 2 3 4 5	1 2 3 4 5
Consistent product quality		1 2 3 4 5	1 2 3 4 5
On-time delivery		1 2 3 4 5	1 2 3 4 5
Accurate invoices		1 2 3 4 5	1 2 3 4 5
Lowest prices		1 2 3 4 5	1 2 3 4 5
Attractive credit terms		1 2 3 4 5	1 2 3 4 5
Salespeople's skills		1 2 3 4 5	1 2 3 4 5
Helpful dispatchers		1 2 3 4 5	1 2 3 4 5
Courteous drivers		1 2 3 4 5	1 2 3 4 5
Supplier resolves problems fairly and quickly		1 2 3 4 5	1 2 3 4 5

Please write in any other items not listed above which are very important to you in making your purchase decision: _____

_____

_____

Response to special needs   Salespeople's skills
Ease of placing orders   Helpful dispatchers
Consistent product quality   Courteous drivers
Accurate invoices   Address problems fairly and quickly
Lowest prices

Customers rank these factors according to how much they influence the decision to purchase from one concrete supplier rather than another. The survey ends with an open-ended question about what customers like and dislike about Granite Rock. If a customer ranks something as important, the company turns its attention to it.

The customer report card and the needs survey are used to create a four-quadrant graph (Figure 6-5) so that Granite Rock employees can see at a glance how they compare to competitors on various quality-related factors.

Grades are on the horizontal axis and importance factors are on the vertical axis. Each axis is the industry average.

Considerations above the center line are more important than items below the line. Items to the left are below the average competitor, ratings to the right are above.

Greg Diehl notes: "We place great emphasis on what is above and below the line in importance. We want to overperform competitors on what is on the top half. That doesn't mean that we don't have to perform on the things that fall below the line. It is not an absolute scale. Some customers judge on the first two items, others want you to have all of the things that they rated [as important]."

Granite Rock keeps down the cost of its surveys by developing

Figure 6-5. Granite Rock: four-quadrant graph.

High Importance

Weakness   Strength

F ———————————————————— A

Not Important   Good

Low Importance

the format and doing the analysis themselves. Diehl emphasizes that surveys don't need to be fancy in order to be effective. You can send a letter instead of a formal survey to ask "what are we doing wrong" and "what are we doing right."

Granite Rock is so committed to customer satisfaction that the company guarantees it. If for any reason a customer is dissatisfied with the company's products or services, they can simply not pay the bill.

Not surprisingly, dissatisfaction is rare. The costs incurred by Granite Rock to resolve customer complaints are equivalent to 0.2 percent of sales, compared with an industry average of 2 percent. And in a fiercely competitive marketplace, revenue per employee at Granite Rock is about 30 percent above the national industry average.

• *Accompanying salespeople on face-to-face calls.* Another way to monitor salespeople's progress in achieving quality is to go on sales calls with them. By traveling with your salespeople, you can see them in action with the customer, observe the steps they take to meet customer expectations, and help them to correct deficiencies in this area, by coaching them after the visit. This is an effective way of maintaining quality control.

• *Incorporating quality into performance reviews.* Make quality issues an integral part of performance reviews. That means that at least some of the performance factors measured in employee reviews should be related to customer satisfaction. For example, responsiveness to customer inquiries is a quality-related performance factor.

Remember, it is the customer who sets quality standards. So the salesperson should be graded on how responsive he or she has been from the customer's point of view. For example, if a customer requests that an order be filled within three days, the salesperson should be judged on whether or not he or she meets this deadline, even if it represents an exceptionally fast turnaround time from the salesperson's point of view.

• *Measuring territory development.* An indirect way of measuring customer satisfaction (and thus salespeople's quality performance) is by measuring territory development. The emphasis in corporate America on short-term profits can impede long-term territory development by encouraging salespeople to go for the quick sale rather than focusing on building customer relationships. But long-term relationships are a primary indicator of satisfied customers, so territory development must be emphasized and measured.

Two key measures of territory development are repeat business and attrition of accounts. If a salesperson is consistently focusing on meeting and exceeding customer expectations, repeat business should be high and attrition low. Another way to gauge salespeople's efforts to satisfy customers is to measure the number of customer focus groups they conduct each quarter.

• *Benchmarking other sales organizations.* Finally, you can measure the success of your salespeople's quality efforts by benchmarking other sales organizations that are considered to be quality leaders. How do the leaders manage to exceed customer expectations? What techniques do they use? What programs do they have in place? What problems did they have to overcome, and how did they overcome them? Study what they do to maintain and improve quality, then measure your own performance against theirs.

How do you find companies to benchmark and get the detailed information you need to determine how your salespeople measure up? One way is to join a professional organization such as Sales and Marketing Executives International. By networking with members, you will quickly find out which sales managers and companies are the quality leaders.

Another way to find benchmark companies is to analyze your salespeople's Won/Lost reports for the previous year. If you find that business is consistently being lost to one or two firms, it may be that these are quality leaders.

• *Providing continuous feedback.* In addition to measuring salespeople's performance as it relates to customer satisfaction, provide them with continuous feedback. This can be done in conjunction with the monthly feedback you give them on their progress in meeting quarterly goals (see Chapter 3).

Process Improvement Tools

There are several process improvement tools you can use to close the gap between customer expectations and salespeople's performance. The Progressive Goal Management system, outlined in Chapter 3, is one such tool. By encouraging salespeople to add customer-focused goals to their quarterly list, you reinforce the need for continuous quality improvement.

Training is another important process improvement tool. If salespeople fall short in any performance standards related to exceeding customer expectations, provide them with training to overcome their deficiencies.

Phil Crosby, who pioneered the quality concept of "zero defects," believes in preventing quality problems at the end of a process by building quality into the front end. In sales, that means training salespeople in identifying needs and providing information that will prevent objections from arising later in the selling process.

Some sales managers feel that training takes away from valuable selling time and makes it tougher for salespeople to achieve their quotas. Training does take time away from selling, but it makes the time that's left more effective. Training makes it easier for reps to achieve their quotas, because it improves their ability to uncover customer needs and meet them.

Also, training doesn't have to take much time away from the field. Rather than hold a two- or three-day seminar once or twice a year, piggyback brief quality training sessions onto other major events, such as trade shows, that sales reps attend.

Choose a topic in quality selling, such as "Meeting and Beating Customer Expectations" or "Developing High-Quality Sales Proposals." Hold a half-day seminar on the topic before the trade show or sales meeting. Six of these half-day seminars scattered throughout the year will be far more effective than a single two- or three-day seminar that reps will soon forget.

Make sure the topic is relevant to the training needs of your salespeople. To ensure this, ask salespeople to offer their suggestions for topics.

Make sure that the topic is timely as well. For example, if the training session is to be held just prior to a trade show, the topic might center around "what trade show attendees want from an exhibitor." By training sales reps in advance of an event in a topic that is relevant to the event, they get a chance to practice their skills immediately, which reinforces their learning.

Training is as important for veteran salespeople as for novices. Salespeople who started out twenty years ago may not have had training in a decade. What they believe to be customer-focused behavior may be very different from the customer's perception. As discussed in Chapter 7, the well-entrenched "sales-driven" style of selling does not focus on the customer but on making the sale by using manipulative techniques. Training can help to change the sales-driven mind set to one that is customer-focused.

Rewards

What gets rewarded gets done, so it's important to reward salespeople for their quality efforts. Earlier I discussed the need to conduct customer surveys to find out how well salespeople are meeting customer expectations. Reward those salespeople who received the highest scores from customers by giving them a bonus or a trip at the end of the year. This reinforces the idea that your company acknowledges and appreciates quality efforts.

Many company commission plans emphasize getting new orders. To reward territory development (and the long-term customer satisfaction that it implies), give a bonus for repeat business. You can also offer bonuses or awards at the end of the year to those reps who are most successful in keeping existing customers satisfied, whether or not the customers placed an order that year.

Four Cultural Elements Required for Total Quality Selling

Quality programs will take root and blossom only if the cultural environment is favorable for them. What kind of corporate culture encourages Total Quality Selling? One in which workers are empowered, communication lines are wide open, the entire company is committed to quality, and there is strong leadership at the top of the sales organization and the entire company.

Empowerment

Chapter 3 discusses the need to empower salespeople, to give them broad responsibility and authority to make decisions on the use of resources (within their control) to secure business. It stresses the need for the sales manager to support salespeople's direction and efforts but not to monitor their every movement.

An empowering environment gives salespeople the decision-making tools to provide total customer satisfaction. The stories of a controlling manager and an empowering manager will show how empowerment helps salespeople to meet and exceed customer expectations, whereas controlling them inhibits their ability to do so.

The controlling manager, Dave, works for a chemical manufacturer, called, in this example, Chemical Products. He requires his salespeople to justify at the beginning of each week every item on their weekly schedule. Eventually his salespeople become extremely dependent on him to make decisions on all activities and use of resources for them.

Jennifer is an empowering manager working for Ajax Computer Manufacturers. She lets her salespeople visit whomever they want during the week. And she gives them the authority and responsibility to make decisions, including major decisions that have a serious impact on the business.

When a Chemical Products customer experienced a crisis—an unscheduled shutdown of a major piece of equipment—he asked one of Dave's salespeople, who had sold him the equipment: "What do you intend to do?" The rep's response was: "Let me talk to my manager." It took one full day to track down Dave, who was on the road with another sales rep. Dave authorized a tech support person to fly out to visit the customer, who by now was very upset because close to a full day of production was lost.

Contrast this with how one of Jennifer's salespeople handled a crisis with a key customer. An Ajax computer was dead on arrival at the customer's site. The Ajax rep, without consulting Jennifer, immediately started the wheels turning to get the defective product returned and replaced with a new product. The system was in place the next day.

Which of the two companies do you think has the most satisfied customers?

Open Communications

Chapter 2 discusses the importance of open communications to maintain a productive, high-energy, high-morale environment.

Open communications are also critical to creating an environment for Total Quality Selling.

If they are to achieve continuous improvement, salespeople must feel free to speak openly about quality problems. When a sales rep observes an inconsistency in a TQS practice, he or she must be able to speak out about it without fear of retaliation.

Different companies use different methods of promoting open communications. Some use forms to record quality problems; the forms are then sent to the people responsible for solving the problem. Other companies, such as General Electric, have "workout groups," meetings during which all employees can voice their concerns to upper management.

Having observed and used both methods of getting employees involved in solving quality problems, I believe that neither is adequate alone. Filling out paperwork that is not directly related to sales numbers is a difficult activity to reinforce or promote among salespeople. Workout groups or roundtables in which salespeople bring their concerns to management are effective to a limited extent. But if these meetings are held only quarterly, there will be a buildup of concerns among some salespeople and others will forget the problems they intended to bring up.

The best approach is to make quality problem solving an ongoing process rather than confining it to periodic quality meetings. For the goal of continuous improvement to be achieved, salespeople must play an integral role in solving problems as they arise.

When salespeople observe a quality-related problem, make certain they communicate their concern to whomever is responsible for solving the problem. To assure satisfactory problem resolution, set up a problem tickler file. Whenever a quality problem occurs, have your reps phone your administrator or coordinator and give him or her the following information:

- Description of the problem
- Name of the person who was contacted about the problem
- Date the problem was reported

Have your administrator type up the information in a report and put it in your tickler file. Each week, let all salespeople know (via memo or voice mail) about quality problems that have been reported and those that have been solved. This reinforces the fact that you are committed to Total Quality Selling.

If the problem is one that the salesperson can solve, follow up each week with the rep to determine the status of the problem. If, after a specified period of time, the rep indicates the problem has not been solved, you should then take over so that the rep is freed to continue his or her selling activities.

By allowing and encouraging your salespeople to speak out about quality problems and making it clear that they will not be punished for doing so, you will reinforce the need for continuous improvement.

Companywide Commitment to Quality

Total Quality requires a companywide commitment. The sales department must team up with the rest of the company in order to reach its own quality goals. Part of the sales manager's job is to act as a coordinator, to make certain that salespeople work with other departments to solve quality-related problems, share suggestions for improvements, and achieve quality-related goals.

How can the sales team work with other departments when they have independent goals? The answer depends on how closely the sales manager promotes the values and corporate mission of the company. Sales meetings are a good place to start.

In one of my sales management positions, I solicited the vice presidents of finance, engineering, and manufacturing to complete a brief questionnaire about their job responsibilities and the major improvements needed in their departments.

From the questionnaires, I compiled a profile of each executive and invited them all to attend one of our sales meetings to observe our team-building exercises. In these exercises, one team of four salespeople took on the role of vice president of manufacturing, another would assume the role of vice president of engineering, and so on. The teams' job was to read the profiles I'd compiled from the questionnaires and think up ways to solve the major quality problems of their respective departments.

These team exercises were highly productive. The salespeople not only produced some excellent suggestions that were already being tried by the various departments (which impressed the VPs), but because they were outsiders, they were able to offer fresh ideas that the department managers hadn't considered.

The results of these team exercises reinforced the fact that salespeople, even though located miles away from headquarters, can contribute to helping the rest of the company to make continuous quality improvements. This makes the salespeople feel more committed to working as a team with the rest of the company, it gives the members of other departments an appreciation of salespeople's skills, and it strengthens the company's overall quality efforts.

Leadership at the Top

For Total Quality Selling to become a way of life, there must be strong leadership from the sales manager and from the CEO. The leadership of the organization must spell out the vision of Total Quality to all employees, then provide them with the tools, support, guidance, and encouragement they need to achieve the vision. Most importantly, they must demonstrate quality so that employees have a model to follow.

People learn best by example. Unless the leaders of the organization practice (not just preach) Total Quality in their own positions, they won't succeed in convincing employees to practice continuous improvement in their jobs.

As a sales manager, you cannot force the CEO to practice Total Quality Management. But you can create a quality environment within your sales organization and set an example for the rest of the company. Once other managers begin to observe the power of Total Quality Selling, they will follow your lead and begin to incorporate quality efforts into their own departments.

No matter how committed the organization's leadership is to the concept of quality, implementing Total Quality is a slow and sometimes painful process that often requires deep attitudinal, behavioral, and cultural changes. Such changes are not made overnight. But they are well worth the time and commitment involved. The following case studies include the stories of two companies—Baxter Health Care and Motorola Corporation—who have successfully implemented quality programs in their sales organizations.

Case Studies: Implementing Quality in the Sales Organization

THE BAXTER QUALITY SALES PROCESS

Baxter Health Care manufactures and distributes more than 120,000 hospital supply and scientific products worldwide. With $9 billion in annual revenues, the company is one of the world's largest manufacturers and distributors of health care products.

In the early 1980s, Baxter Health Care began a major quality improvement effort, dubbed the Quality Leadership Process (QLP). The program has been implemented in virtually all of Baxter's manufacturing plants. Now the company is moving the program into its sales organization.

Following are excerpts from a conversation with Rick Salzer, Baxter's director of marketing for corporate sales and marketing, about how his company is implementing quality in the sales force.

Question: What made you decide to implement a total quality program in your sales organization?

Salzer: Over the last two years, we decided that it made a lot of sense for our salespeople to be able to work within the same type of quality process that we have implemented in our manufacturing plants. We feel that the time is right, in terms of what's going on in health care reform, for us to look at our approach to the customer in a different light, and this is a terrific way to do that.

Our customers— hospitals—started down the quality road before our sales teams did. In fact, they are being mandated by their accreditation organization to have a quality process, and they're implementing it at a fast rate. We wanted to make sure we understood what they were doing, as well as to be able to work in an environment that applied quality every day, within the hospital and within the supplier or supply chain.

So a couple of years ago, a task force was created to take our Quality Leadership Process and tailor it for the sales force, to create case studies and tools and a "how to" manual on how to take our TQM program from manufacturing, put it in the hands of salespeople, and apply it to a customer relationship.

Q: Would you say the driving force for implementing Total Quality in the sales arena was the hospitals' need for accreditation?

A: I would say the driving force for us was the need to do a better job with our customers. They're demanding more of us than they have in the past, and they're asking us to assist them in ways that we've never been asked to before. They're looking at us as a resource, and for us to be able to do that, we needed some new tools to teach our salespeople, so that they would be as effective and productive as possible with the customer.

The old ways of selling aren't going to cut it anymore. We need to be right out in front with things that are going to help our customers.

It's a shrinking market place. There are fewer hospitals today than there were last year, there are fewer inpatients. The amount of money that insurance companies and the Federal Government is willing to pay is going down. So you've got a constricted revenue stream. And you've got more and more competition. What we try to do is assist our customers in that difficult environment. It's a question of productivity. To drive productivity you need quality, and that's where we're coming from with this.

Q: How is the implementation progressing?

A: To date we've developed the "how to" manual. We call it the Baxter Quality Sales Process. We're in the process of teaching this process to 2,500 salespeople across the United States. This will involve the largest training program Baxter's ever done for the sales force.

Approximately forty of what we call our corporate account executives have already been trained in it. They and their management teams have already gone through the process and are working with it with corporate customers right now. Corporate customers are a subset of the domestic marketplace. We have allocated extra resources for these customers because they represent some of the biggest and most active hospitals and hospital systems in the country.

By the end of this year, all of our domestic sales forces will have been trained on QSP and will be working with virtually all 6,000 U.S. hospitals. Our expectation is that when they come out of this, all of these salespeople will have a good understanding of basic quality tools, but with a salesperson's slant on them. They will be better able to understand what their customers' requirements are and to come up with tools, techniques, and processes to satisfy, exceed, and, in today's term, "delight" the customer by exceeding their expectations.

Q: Can you give more of the details of the Baxter Quality Sales Process?

A: The Quality Sales Process is a teamwork approach to quality in the sales force that focuses on determining customer requirements, understanding them, and then using TQM tools to satisfy those requirements. Each team consists of sales representatives and managers from any division of Baxter that wants to participate in that particular account and anyone else who can aid the process. We have had teams as large as fifty people. This could be customer service people, but it can also be the person who drives the truck or the person who works on the forklift, staging orders for some of our special distribution programs for customers.

Our corporate account executives are given the role of functioning as the key contact for hospital administration. And we try to have a different member of our team working in each part of the hospital.

Q: Who decides which hospitals to approach in a team fashion?

A: Our corporate account executives are the people who make the decision about where we're going to start with this process. We're in the third year now. Nationwide, we choose ninety different accounts each year. It is very time-consuming, but once the approach is learned by the members of the team, the skills that they've acquired are transferred to hospitals that aren't participating in this process.

Q: How do you initiate the Quality Process with a customer?

A: We sit down with a customer at the beginning of the year (actually, it could be virtually any time) and say, "We believe we have resources that can help you. Consider us as a partner, not necessarily a supplier of lab products or IV solutions or OR products. Tell us what you are trying to accomplish as a hospital organization." And we may hear things like "reduce operating expenses," "implement a continuous quality improvement process within our hospital," or "maintain a competitive edge over the other hospital competitors in town."

We list all of these goals on paper, and we also ask the customer to define the requirements necessary to reach those goals. And as we are defining the requirements, we put a process in place that provides for an understanding of those requirements and an expectation of what's going to happen. "How is this process going to work? What's the desired outcome? By what period of time? Who is going to be responsible for meeting your requirements?" We put the responsibility for following up and measuring how well we accomplished our goals, with the help of the customer, in the hands of the corporate account executive.

Then, we tell the customer about *our* goals. Our goals may be to show that we can differentiate our services with our distribution division, increase the effectiveness of our Baxter team, try to show some of the value-added services we have, and then just look at enhancing our overall account relationship.

Next, we put our goals and the customer's goals on a matrix and say, "Where do our goals line up?" We try to pick the ones with the best "fit" or the ones that we all feel comfortable with and look toward coming up with a requirement worksheet or list of requirements to satisfy those goals.

We rank those goals in importance, set up a time frame, and establish a completion date. And we'll put that all down on paper and leave it to the hospital and the account executive to come up with the score board or measurement system.

Q: What happens after that?

A: The team gets together to put a plan in place to meet the customer's requirements. Once the plan is in place, smaller teams go to work with the individual hospital departments. Issues are identified, root causes found, and solutions developed to positively impact each department or process. Customers are very active participants on these teams.

Q: How have customers responded to the teamwork approach?

A: They're very pleased to see Baxter, which is a pretty large corporation and sometimes difficult to deal with because we have so many different divisions, become more responsive. It's a lot easier for them to deal with somebody they see today, have that person answer all their questions about all the divisions right now, instead of having to make fifteen phone calls to fifteen different Baxter people.

Team members are empowered. If they see a problem, they own it and solve it as best they can and get all the help from the team that they can. We've cut through a lot of the bureaucracy. That's been a real benefit to our customers and our field organization.

Q: Has cross-divisional communication improved as a result of the team approach?

A: Definitely. We have seen our salespeople not only involve their product manager, but go to the members of their team and say, "I need to be able to contact this doctor, this nurse, this department head. Who among our team has a relationship and would be willing to introduce me and help me move my process forward so that the customer, our team, and Baxter wins?

"My goals may be the ones we're trying to accomplish today; yours may be the ones we're trying to achieve tomorrow. You may not, as a sales representative from a different division, have a lot to gain from this introduction, this time. But if we work together as a team, this will help you. We'll have the opportunity to work together and I'll be able to introduce you to someone I know, or provide you with some information that you may need."

Q: How do you balance the need to develop long-term customer relationships with the need to produce short-term profits?

A: It's difficult. In the short term this process takes some extra time and effort from the members of the team. But the increased communication between members of the team and the customer helps us better understand what the customer needs. We can help with answers in terms of products or systems that we offer.

In the long term we have found that customers that develop long-term relationships with us, or with any other supplier, tend to treat that supplier a little differently. In a long-term relationship, customers get comfortable with us. They understand what Baxter's capabilities are and are willing to utilize our value-added services more than customers who don't understand us quite as well. So we end up achieving our short-term goals and building long-term relationships.

If you look at the whole supplier/customer chain, it's basically a continuum. Customers move down this continuum from a transactional relationship to a strategic relationship. As they get toward the more strategic side, they begin to talk in terms of value versus price. Once we've spent some time with customers and they're able to see that, not only do we have competitive prices, but we have other services that they can take advantage of. Then, we really begin to see the relationship take off and both parties benefit more than they have in the past.

Q: How does the sales manager fit into the Quality Sales Process?

A: If the team feels that they need management support, somebody to work with corporate headquarters to bring resources to the customer's assistance, that's where the sales manager's going to fit. He or she is going to find resources to assist the team and the customer and help to facilitate the process wherever possible, as well as manage and train those representatives who aren't working in the team work process yet.

Q: Does senior management have an active role in the process?

A: To make the quality process work, one of the first things you have to have is an executive level commitment. The senior management team has to believe that TQM works. Ours does, because we've seen the results on the manufacturing side and now on the sales side.

Our president and CEO, Jim Tobin, has been one of the key drivers throughout the whole Quality Leadership Process. And he's just as much behind the Quality Sales Process, because we see the value in taking this type of approach to our customers. Our two executive vice presidents, Lester Knight and Tony White, as well as our senior vice president for corporate sales and marketing, Terry Mulligan, have all invested a lot of time in making the Quality Sales Process a success.

Q: How have salespeople reacted to the teamwork concept? After all, salespeople are an autonomous breed.

A: Yes, they are. But it's interesting to see that once you're able to get some success stories and some positive results from this type of approach, it gets a lot easier.

We provided some incentives to these folks initially. We found that the incentive was a great way to kick it off. Since then, the results have sustained the process.

Even though most salespeople are very autonomous, they are also very goal-oriented. Having team members there to assist them in reaching their goals, covering for them when they're away, and, most importantly, assisting the customer, really helps persuade people.

Remember, these folks are still compensated on what they sell to the hospital. So when they can see positive results from account to account, year to year, they become sold on the process. And then they sell the teamwork process to their peers. As a result, we find that instead of having twenty-seven divisions of Baxter, the customer really sees one Baxter.

CUSTOMER NEEDS ANALYSIS AT MOTOROLA

Like Baxter Health Care, Motorola, Inc. is well known for its commitment to quality. As part of that commitment, one of the company's five businesses, the Land Mobile Products sector (LMPS) has developed a Customer Needs Analysis process in order to help customers identify their communications problems and develop solutions with the help of Motorola products. The LMPS manufactures two-way voice and data radio communication systems. With revenues of $4 billion, this sector accounted for nearly a third of Motorola's worldwide sales in 1992 ($13 billion).

At the heart of Customer Needs Analysis is the concept of process mapping, which is an analytical tool that provides a systematic look at how an organization's functions and departments interrelate throughout the stages of a particular process. Cross-functional process mapping details the steps in the process and identifies who performs each one. The object of a process map is to capture and record how a particular input is currently processed—that is, how it is converted from initial input into a final output. The map can also be used to identify and correct critical business problems within and between departments and functions.

Kathy Adomaitis and Linda Lovett, senior project supervisors with Motorola's National Training Team, were responsible for developing the Customer Needs Analysis process. Both are certified in process mapping techniques. Their task was to apply process mapping to the sales environment in the LMPS in order to strengthen customer relationships.

In general, a Needs Analysis is performed for current customers who have been using Motorola products for a limited number of applications. After proving the reliability of its products and service on a small scale, the LMPS approaches customers with the idea of conducting a Needs Analysis to determine how Motorola can provide more comprehensive solutions to their communications problems.

The Customer Needs Analysis process involves five phases (summarized in Figures 6-A through 6-E):

1. Project planning meetings
2. Interviews with key customer personnel and surveys of customer processes
3. Analysis of findings
4. Process mapping
5. Team recommendations

The Needs Analysis Team consists of a sales representative and an engineer, with Marketing and Finance providing assistance as needed. Two people from the customer organization also participate on the team—usually a department head and a functional sponsor, often the director of quality.

By design, the team forms for thirty days and then disbands. The idea is that if an analysis cannot be completed during this time frame, the salesperson has taken on too big a task.

After completing the Customer Needs Analysis, the team presents its findings to an ad hoc task force put together by the customer. Usually, the customer members of the team make the presentation, with the Motorola members available to answer questions and provide support.

Following is a condensed version of a report of the findings of a team formed to conduct a Needs Analysis for Acme. The study was conducted at the request of Jim Johnson, Acme's quality manager.

Background. Acme, established in 1904, is the largest producer of packaged dried foods in the United States. There are many different brands packaged and shipped from the facility under study. The process—from receiving the raw materials, to packaging, to labelling and shipping—covers a wide physical area in several separate locations.

Figure 6-A. Phase one.

Phase One	Who to Involve	Objectives	Outputs	Tools
• Motorola project planning meeting	• Account manager • Other Motorolans, as deemed necessary by the account manager	• Identify potential opportunity. • Develop hypothesis that improved communications can improve business processes. • Determine benefits to customer for performing customer needs analysis. • Develop a meeting with the account strategy.	• High-level view of the account's processes • High-level view of account's goals • Hypothesis of how customer's core business processes interrelate • Meeting strategy to include: — hypothesis — project scope — project requirements — project deliverables	• Account planning forms • Company literature — annual report — news articles • Sample overheads
• Customer meeting	• Account manager • Customer and/or customer team	• Set/manage customer's expectations. • Obtain customer's commitment to participate. • Gain commitment for access to resources. — people to interview — time for interviews	• Commitment to proceed	• Customized version of the sample over-heads

These assorted processes require constant and continuous communications. The variety of customer needs, the importance of quality, and the variety of products and product configurations contribute to the complexity of the processes.

There is no question that each department is dependent upon the others to achieve a totally satisfied customer. To ensure this goal, all departments need to have continuous, real-time communications.

To ensure their needs are being met, the people who work at the facility must be asked about the details of their job requirements, with respect to communications. From this information, gaps or deficiencies in current and future communications can be identified. By analyzing the causes of these deficiencies, appropriate communications solutions can prescribed.

The Motorola Needs Analysis Team was composed of the following people:

Jane Doe	Motorola Regional Manager
Tom Jones	Motorola Account Manager
Tim Smith	Motorola Account Executive

In addition, two representatives from Acme participated on the team to champion the analysis and review the recommendations: Jim Johnson, Acme's quality manager, mentioned earlier, and Karen James, vice president of operations for Acme.

Phase One: Project Planning Meetings. The first Customer Needs Analysis Team meeting was conducted at Motorola, with all the Motorola people who would be involved in the analysis in attendance. During this meeting, the project plan was revised and accountability for all activities was assigned. Following the meeting, a presentation to the Customer Team members was given.

The purpose of this meeting was to obtain commitment to proceed, identify the strategic processes to target, and identify the key personnel within each Acme department to interview during the allotted time frame (thirty days).

In order to prepare the key personnel for their interviews, Acme, working with the Needs Analysis Team, developed and distributed communications questionnaires to them. These questionnaires

(Text continues on page 149)

Figure 6-B. Phase two.

Phase Two	Who to Involve	Objectives	Outputs	Tools
• Interviews with key personnel	• Account manager • Customer contact or champion	• Using initial hypothesis, identify key function representatives who need to be interviewed. • Using initial hypothesis, determine what information needs to be gathered. • Develop typical question set. • Test hypothesis against information gathered. Adjust if necessary.	• List of interviewees with dates and times for interviews • Information flows (inputs and outputs) identified for each function • List of additional information that might be needed (i.e., any additional departments you uncovered that should be interviewed)	• Organizational chart • Sample question set

| • Survey actual process | • Account manager
• Functional representatives from customer's organization | • Visually understand customer's process.

• Validate the information flow process.
• Identify process improvement points that the customer may not be aware of.

• Gather and record specific radio operational information that might be used later in the process. | • Physical walk-throughs of functional operations conducted
• Validated interview data
• List of obstacles, barriers, etc., to the customer's process
— visual limitations
— environmental constraints
— noise factors
• List of specific radio system operational concerns | • Walk-through |

Figure 6-C. Phase three.

Phase Three	Who to Involve	Objectives	Outputs	Tools
• Analysis of the findings	• Account manager • Other Motorolans, as deemed necessary by the account manager	• Categorize the data into areas where improved communication technology would improve the business processes. • Interpret the data into communications technology building blocks. • Formulate conceptual solution.	• List of findings tied to customer benefits (observations/findings/ conclusions) • Conceptual solution identified.	• Sample analysis worksheets

Figure 6-D. Phase four.

Phase Four	Who to Involve	Objectives	Outputs	Tools
• Map the process	• Account manager • Other Motorolans, as deemed necessary by the account manager	• Convey understanding of the customer's business processes. • Graphically represent the relationship between functions—how information flows through the organization. • Identify gaps or disconnects in the information flow process. • Pinpoint critical processes where improved communications can improve the overall business operation (cycle time, quality, process improvements, etc.). • Construct a cross-functional process map of that process.	• High-level relationship map (level 1 map) • Cross-functional key process map (level 2 map)	• Suggested reading: "Improving Performance," Geary Rummler & Alan Brache • Synopsis of mapping • Sample of process maps

Figure 6-E. Phase five.

Phase Five	Who to Involve	Objectives	Outputs	Tools
• Committee recommenda-tions	• Account manager • Other Motorolans, as deemed necessary by the account manager • Customer's project committee	• Share information on customer's business processes. • Present conceptual ideas in terms of how im-proved communications can improve overall business operations. • Recommend a process for moving forward. • Gain customer's com-mitment.	• Revised process maps • Summary of observa-tions/findings/conclu-sions • Permission to proceed with technical needs analysis	• Sample Customer Needs Analysis Report

helped focus the employees' thoughts about current communications systems, relative to their job responsibilities. The responses to the questionnaires were invaluable in helping the team to understand the current communications systems within each department.

Phase Two: Interviews With Key Personnel and Surveys of Acme Processes. Questions were established by the Motorola Customer Needs Analysis Team to determine information flows. These questions were used in conjunction with the interview process. The questions were divided into four categories:

1. Job function information
2. Current communications
3. Radio specific information
4. Safety and environmental issues

Following is a sample of questions in each category:

Job Function Information

- What is the central mission of your group?
- What is the input to your department?
- What do you do with this input?
- Are your people on the move?
- Is there any part of the process that is time intensive? Labor intensive? Equipment intensive?
- Do your people need input from any other department?
- What happens if the information arrives early/late?
- Where does your output go?
- What is the key business issue that keeps you up at night?
- If you have a magic wand and could change one thing about the way you communicate information, what would it be?

Current Communications

- How important is it that your communications be secure?
- How long are typical phone conversations?
- Would a centrally staffed point for communications control or management be beneficial to your operations? How?
- Do you have isolated or remote locations?

- How do your people currently access your computer system and databases when they are away from your premises? Is there a need to do so?

Radio Specific Information

- Do you currently use two-way radio? Paging?
- What do you use it for?
- Finish this sentence: "If I could get my system to do _____ , I would use it more."
- Does sharing a frequency with other businesses represent a risk to you?

Safety/Environmental Issues

- How do you currently provide after-hours security for small, unattended sites in your operation?
- How do people currently request emergency assistance from isolated or remote locations?
- How do workers currently notify managers/foreman of emergency situations?
- Who is designated to respond to requests for emergency help via radio?

During the interviews, information flows were identified and communications data regarding department job duties and tasks were collected. These interviews allowed for a deeper understanding of the current types of communications within Acme's departments and key processes and the types of communications tools currently used.

A physical walk-through of Acme's facility was conducted to better understand the business processes and communications flows. Walk-throughs were conducted in the following areas: warehouse, shipping, packaging, and yard control. Observations and interviews with key personnel provided additional input regarding key issues, such as the critical need to communicate with people in different locations and time-critical issues.

By observing the line runs, several environmental obstacles to communications were identified, such as:

- Phones not easily accessible
- Noise

- Distance
- Length of line
- Visual limitations

Phase Three: Analysis of Findings. As part of the data analysis phase, categories were established to reflect where improved communications technology would improve the business processes within Acme. These categories were as follows:

- Quality improvement
- Reduced risk related to safety, security, environment
- Need for improved communications between functions
- Current communications methods not working
- Specific process points where communications would have high impact
- Projects under consideration that are focused on improving processes

Observations/Findings/Conclusions. Throughout the analysis process, the Customer Needs Analysis team focused on three critical processes: materials, shipping, and production planning. Although all three are vital to the success of Acme, it became apparent that the Production Planning Department drives all the other processes.

Other Key Observations

- *The manufacturing processes are not static.* They are subject to constant changes based on many different factors, such as changing forecasts, availability of product, arrivals of just-in-time materials, and quality checks. Any one of these changes can cause serious downstream effects for the remainder of the facility, if not communicated quickly and efficiently. There is a critical need for "real time" communications between the various functions.

- *Packaging and shipping operations are highly interdependent.* What happens in one area of the process seriously affects the operation of the other area. For example, the line that takes the materials from one location to the other is very long and travels between several different floors and through several different buildings. It is often difficult to spot a problem until it has become a major issue. These problems could be avoided by enhancing the communications between the different functions. There is a critical need for improved communications between functions.

▪ At several different places, it was noted that *individuals were running from place to place quite often*. Whether it was from different places on the line to the telephone, or from one end of the building to the other to locate a supervisor, a great deal of time seemed to be spent running around the buildings. When questioned about where they were going, most employees replied that it was critical to notify someone of something that was happening in the process. The failure to notify in a timely manner would cause a defect. If there were a more efficient way to communicate this information, individuals would have more time to attend to fixing the problems. Therefore, it appears that improved communications could significantly reduce defects in the processes.

▪ *When a major problem does occur, it usually requires leaving the scene to physically locate someone, or locate a telephone in order to page for help.* Once the page has been received, the person paged must return the call for more detailed information. From observations and interviews, it was found that most often, the person initiating the call either leaves the site to fix the problem, or stays on the line to continue to notify others of the trouble. As a result, the person who has been paged does not get through, or when he or she does, the phone continues to ring, as no one is nearby to answer it. This creates an enormous amount of wasted time and effort, in addition to causing downstream effects of not fixing the problem. It was apparent that the existing communications methods are not providing the functionality required to communicate quickly and effectively.

▪ *There are many places where there are potential safety and security risks.* Because the campus covers a large geographic are, there are times when employees need to enter dangerous or confined spaces alone, times when technicians must obtain readings from equipment in remote locations, and times when employees may be out of direct contact with other employees.

▪ *Many of Acme's managers currently wear two pagers.* When asked why, the managers responded that the "in-house" paging system did not always meet their needs. Many of these people need to be contacted away from campus, after hours, and the current local area system was not reaching them. It appears that this system needs to be reevaluated in terms of the customer's needs.

▪ In the interviews with various departments, it was discovered that *many departments are investigating alternative means of communicating with each other.* It is not clear to what extent these efforts are being coordinated. There is a need to make certain that these communications methods can be integrated.

Phase Four: Process Mapping. Two process maps are products of this study. The first is a relationship map (Figure 6-F), which graphically shows the relationship between the various functions within Acme and how information currently flows through the customer organization. The second (Figure 6-G) is a cross-functional process map detailing the steps involved from the beginning of the process to the end, i.e., from the time material comes into a plant until it is ready to be shipped.

Phase Five: Team Recommendations. There is a clear need for a plant-wide communication system. The recommendation of this team is to develop one common communication pipeline. This would ensure the integration of different communications systems and would allow for consistency of information flow throughout the Acme facility.

Once the main pipeline has been identified, different communications needs of organizational subsystems can be met. For example, some departments will need portables, some paging, some hand-held data terminals, and so on. However, the main pipeline is what provides the interface between the different systems and needs of the individual departments within the company.

The key to the success of this project is cross-functional involvement and a common pipeline that meets the needs of all users.

Phase 1 implementation is the design of a communications pipeline that will meet all needs within the Acme facility. Second, Acme will need to prioritize those subsystems that are the most critical business process points. Process maps can help to identify the most critical subsystems. These subsystems can then be implemented to meet those most critical needs.

Phase 2 implementation is the implementation of the various other organizational subsystems. These can be added as the need

(Text continues on page 156)

Figure 6-F. Relationship map.

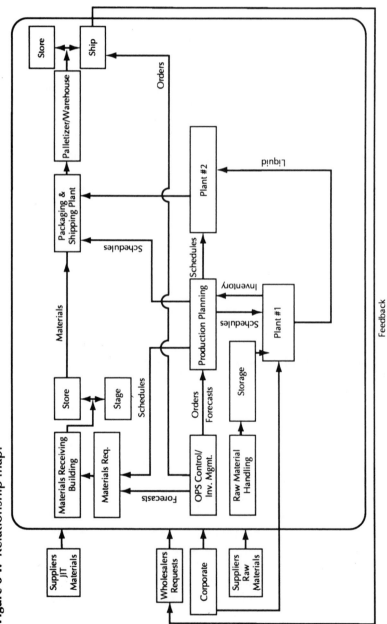

Figure 6-G. Cross-functional process map.

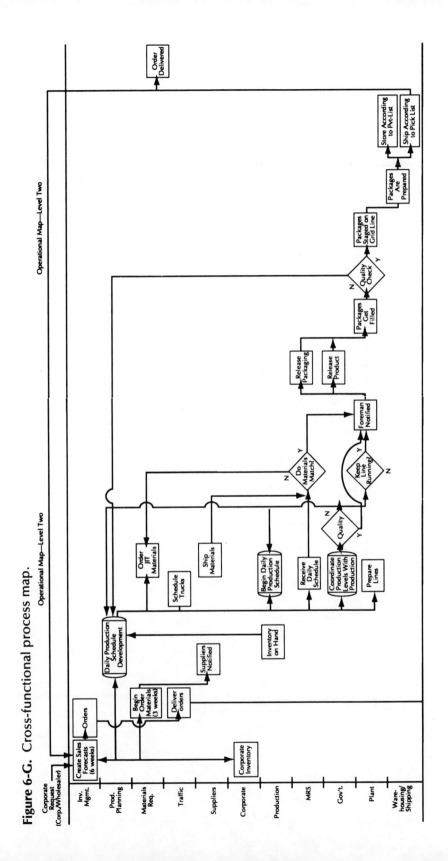

arises or funding becomes available. With the communications pipeline already established, there will be a common interface among additional subsystems.

Many of the departments are currently investigating alternative means for communicating. As they proceed, it is recommended that there be a common funnel, so that as equipment is purchased, it can be integrated into a common pipeline. Perhaps a team should be established to monitor the purchase of communications equipment.

The secret to making Customer Needs Analysis work, according to Kathy Adomaitis, is to "keep the questioning process open enough to capture the unique needs of each customer." Linda Lovett adds: "It's important to concentrate on a critical 'hot spot' that reflects customer's core processes. In a very short time, you'll find important clues to how you can affect the customer's entire operation."

The Customer Needs Analysis process has succeeded in strengthening the relationship between Motorola's Land Mobile Products sector and its customers, according to Tom McCarty, communications and electronics group vice president for Motorola's National Training Team. "Customers involved in the process are telling us that we know more about their business than they do," says McCarty. "When we conduct a Needs Analysis, they perceive us as consultants rather than salespeople. And they view us as real partners in achieving their business goals."

Chapter 7

The Customer-Focused Selling Process

Karen Johnson is the marketing manager for a quality-driven consumer products company. She is thinking about buying a new computer system for her department, because the current system is inflexible, slow, and incompatible with the other computers in the company. Karen has a lot of questions for the four salespeople who are trying to sell her a new system. Among other things, she wants them to explain what makes their systems better than the one the department has now. She wants to know why two of the systems are significantly higher in price than the others. She wants to find out which system will best help her department to achieve its goals of higher productivity and greater responsiveness to customers. She also wants to know if the reps' companies will be around to support the system after the sale.

But Karen doesn't get much chance to ask these questions. The four reps with whom she's been dealing have been doing most of the talking. During the first meeting with one of the reps, Karen spoke for only five minutes; the rep filled the other 25 minutes with a lengthy monologue about his system's features and his company's history.

The rep had stopped by Karen's office without an appointment, interrupting her work day. The only reason she had agreed to see him was that buying a computer system was a high-priority project.

After the first few minutes, it was obvious to Karen that this rep, like the others, was more interested in selling his product than in satisfying her needs. He didn't even make an effort to find out her needs, beyond asking a few "canned" questions, all designed to lead her to choose his product.

The three times when she did manage to interrupt the rep long enough to ask a question, she didn't get a satisfactory answer. For example, when she brought up a concern about the system's capability for networking with other computers, the rep became defensive and began to attack the competition.

The more forcefully the rep touted the superiority of his system over its competitors, the less sincere he sounded and the more wary Karen became about buying anything from him. When he began his high-pressure close, which included a veiled warning that buying from a competitor might result in Karen losing her job, she escorted him out the door.

Karen went back to her office, sat down and heaved a sigh. Her secretary followed her into the office and handed her three messages from the other computer salespeople, who had phoned to find out whether she had made a decision.

One reason Karen hadn't yet made a decision was that she hadn't had time to review the ten-inch stack of product information on her desk. "Evaluating these products could be a full-time job," she thought. She already had more than a full-time job and was having trouble finding extra time to pore over all of the product information and compare the costs and benefits of various systems.

Even if she could find time to go through the mountain of literature left behind by the four salespeople, she would have difficulty doing it without an interpreter. Although Karen considered herself to be fairly computer-literate, the product literature on her desk was filled with technical jargon and buzzwords she didn't understand. And it was virtually impossible to compare the features of the systems, because different vendors described the same features using different terminology. None of the salespeople had bothered to explain the differences in terminology to her.

Karen sighed in exasperation as she opened the product folder at the top of the stack. "This decision had better be the right one," she thought. She knew that her manager was under tremendous pressure to reduce operating costs and boost productivity and quality, and the new system was supposed to be just the thing that would help. She was thankful that she didn't have to make the decision alone; the rest of the committee would have to agree to the purchase.

Sales-Driven vs. Customer-Focused Selling

The above story describes the sales-driven approach to selling. This selling style is characterized by control and manipulation and an adversarial relationship between the salesperson and the customer.

The sales-driven rep has only one goal: to get the order, whether or not the customer needs the product. To get the order, the sales-driven rep will try to control every step of the selling process, avoiding tough questions, ignoring or minimizing objections, and otherwise manipulating the customer into making a decision that is best for the salesperson, but not necessarily for the customer.

Most people have encountered this style of salesperson at one time or another; the sales-driven approach is widely used. But it is gradually being replaced by another, more powerful approach to selling that focuses, not on getting the order, but on satisfying the customer.

The customer-focused approach to selling is the direct opposite of the sales-driven style. The customer-focused salesperson doesn't try to control the customer; rather, the customer is in charge every step of the way. The salesperson acts as a guide or facilitator, helping the customer to refine and communicate his or her needs and to choose the product that will best meet those needs—even if it's a competitor's product (more on that later).

Under the customer-focused approach, the salesperson and the customer are partners rather than adversaries. There is no reason for the salesperson to manipulate the customer, because both are on the same side. Because the rep is focused on serving the customer rather than closing the sale, canned and self-serving questions are eliminated. Ironically, this increases rather than decreases the chances of making the sale.

From this discussion it should be clear that the customer-focused approach is the one that is used by high-quality sales organizations. Chapter 6 notes that quality in the sales organization involves meeting and exceeding customer expectations. The customer-focused selling approach is intended to do just that, in every interaction with the customer. At the end of every step in the selling process, the customer-focused rep checks with the customer to make sure that all of his or her questions and concerns have been addressed satisfactorily, before moving on to the next step.

Technique vs. Process

In an interview with *Training* magazine, Gerhard Gschwandtner, publisher of *Personal Selling Power*, was asked to pinpoint the sales skills necessary for success in the nineties and beyond. He replied that "salespeople must remember to be human beings. The problem with a lot of salespeople is they've been trained to become sales automatons—to sell a standardized product with a standardized approach that uses a routine for questioning and formulas for closing."[1]

He is referring to sales-driven reps. These are the salespeople who rely solely on prepackaged techniques and formulas to win the sale. This is one reason they must control every step of the selling process. If a customer asks a question for which they have no canned response, these reps don't know what to do next.

By contrast, customer-focused salespeople are process-oriented. They don't rely on preset formulas, questions, or techniques; they don't need to. All they must do is concentrate on the process of helping customers to define their needs, then find a way of meeting those needs. This gives them infinitely more flexibility than the sales-driven rep; they can adjust their presentation to suit the needs of the customer rather than rely on preset responses. And it gives them more credibility, since most people see right through canned presentations and manipulative techniques.

Steps in the Selling Process

Sales training companies vary in the terminology they use to describe the selling process, but it boils down to the five following steps:

1. Qualifying
2. Uncovering customer needs
3. Presenting information
4. Handling objections
5. Closing

Each step of the process is handled in distinctly different ways, depending on whether the salesperson is sales-driven or customer-focused. Figure 7-1 summarizes the differences. In the following examples, we contrast the two styles by showing how Don (a sales-driven rep) and Marilyn (a customer-focused rep) approach the selling process. By going step-by-step through the selling process, it will become obvious why customer-focused selling is a superior approach.

Step 1: Qualifying (the Opening Sales Call)

Sales-Driven. Don always opens the first sales call with some small talk. He may see a photo on the desk that shows the customer fishing in a beautiful stream and ask: "How often do you go fishing?" His intent is to build rapport by appealing to the personal interests of the customer.

Once he sees that he has established some rapport, Don proceeds with a series of canned qualifying questions. One of the first questions he asks is: "Who else will be making the buying decision?" The next question is: "How much is he (or she) willing to spend?" The last qualifying question focuses on the uses or applications of the product.

Once Don knows how the customer intends to use the product, he mentally begins to select among his company's products the one that will best match the customer's uses. If the customer says he needs a medical instrument that can do a specific type of test and tells Don his budget is $25,000, Don mentally searches to find such a product. If the closest product

Figure 7-1. Sales-driven vs. customer-focused selling steps.

Sales Steps	Sales-Driven	Customer-Focused
Step 1: Qualification	Superficial interest is shown in customer hobbies. Set agenda of questions.	Precall planning assists in understanding customer's markets and products. Spontaneous dialogue allows salesperson to learn more of customer and business.
Step 2: Uncovering Internal Needs and Learning Buying Process	Questions are asked to verify product selection. Buying process questions are asked to aid in salesperson forecast.	Questions are asked to understand how product will affect the personal welfare of the customer. Buying process questions assist in planning the sequence of steps for the purchase.
Step 3: Presentation	Features rich presentation. Most of the features presented do not relate to customer's surface or internal needs.	Before presenting, salesperson understands how customer wants information presented. Presentation helps customer understand and differentiate.
Step 4: Handling Objections	Presents additional information to neutralize customer's objections or minimizes the importance of customer's objection.	Objections are avoided through effective questioning. Any objections that do arise are resolved by customers.
Step 5: Closing	Salesperson makes decision for customer by using closing techniques.	Salesperson facilitates closing by getting smaller agreements from the customer throughout the entire selling process. These smaller agreements lead to a final decision.

costs $30,000, Don is already thinking about ways he can reduce the price to $25,000.

Don's next few questions are to verify the product selection. He wants to make certain that he understands all of the customer's potential uses so that the recommended product can satisfy tomorrow's needs as well as today's.

All of the questions Don asks are focused on a single objective: making a sale.

Customer-Focused. Before Marilyn goes on her first sales call, she finds out all she can about the customer's business, by reading trade journals and going through the company's annual reports or whatever other information she can find. The purpose of this precall planning is to build her own confidence and to help the customer feel confident that Marilyn knows what she is talking about.

When Marilyn arrives at the customer's office, she also begins the conversation with small talk, but it is focused on the customer's business—the reason she is here, after all. This helps to establish her image as a professional in the eyes of the customer and to develop the customer's trust.

From her precall research, Marilyn learned that the customer's company has just introduced a new product, so she asks him how the product introduction went. This gets him talking about his company and his role in the product introduction. While he is talking, Marilyn is gathering information about his responsibilities in the company, his needs, and his problems, and she is trying to determine whether his needs overlap with any of the products she has to offer.

From the way he discusses his problems, Marilyn also gets a clue about the level of technical detail she should use in presenting information to him (something the sales-driven rep doesn't bother to do).

Marilyn needs to know how the customer plans to go about the buying process, so she asks him who else is involved in the purchase decision (she refers to the purchase "team," which is the language the customer uses). Then she lets the customer speak freely about the various team members. From his discussion, she gathers information about how much influence he has over the decision, what are the needs of the other players on the team, and what she can do to help in the buying process.

When the time comes to ask about funding for the product, Marilyn's first question is not about the size of the budget. Instead, she asks how the budget was set, so she can better understand the customer's point of view. Perhaps the budget was based on the price of a similar product the company purchased six years ago. If so, this signals that the customer may have an unrealistic idea of the current worth of the product. If the budget is based on what the company can afford, and it's clear there is no possibility for additional funding, this is the time for Marilyn to find out what the limit is. If her product is above this budget limit, she knows that she either must find a way to reduce the price, or recognize that she cannot help the customer in this case. This is in contrast to the sales-driven rep, who would try to manipulate the customer into spending more than he was able to pay.

Now that Marilyn has information about the other team members and has established the financial guidelines, she asks the customer about the applications of the product.

If the customer wants to replace an older product, Marilyn asks him to tell her what he likes and dislikes about the current product and, if possible, to demonstrate the product. Such demonstrations are usually a more effective way of determining how the customer applies a product than having him simply describe the applications. And they make the customer feel more comfortable, by putting him in his everyday working environment and giving him a chance to "vent" about the problems he has with the product and talk about what he'd like in the replacement product.

If the customer is buying a new product rather than a replacement, Marilyn asks him to describe a similar product he's read or heard about or used and to tell what he likes or dislikes about the product. This gives her insight into the customer's way of thinking.

Unlike the sales-driven salesperson, at this stage Marilyn is not trying to come up with a product match. She is still trying to understand her customer's needs in as much detail as possible. During this qualifying step, she has uncovered many of her customer's surface needs. In the next step she will focus on the customer's personal needs, his underlying motivations for buying.

Step 2: Uncovering the Customer's Internal Needs And Determining the Buying Process

Sales-Driven. Step 1 focused in part on discussing customer needs and potential product applications. Step 2 goes beyond that to determine *why* certain product features are important to the customer. This involves finding out the customer's deeper motivations.

The first part of this step is all but eliminated in the sales-driven approach. Sales-driven salespeople don't care about finding out customer's true motivations. All they want to do is get enough information about the customer's basic requirements so that they can find a product that matches the requirements and begin to rattle off its features and move into their sales pitch.

Once Don senses that he might get the order, he asks the customer who will be signing the purchase order requisition after he makes a recommendation, whether the paperwork will go to another company site for additional signatures, and how long the process will take. None of these questions are asked for the customer's benefit. They are asked only for Don's benefit, so he'll know when he can expect to close the order and collect his commission.

Customer-Focused. Unlike Don, Marilyn takes the time to uncover the customer's deeper motivations for buying. During the qualification step, customers generally talk about surface needs: how much memory they want in their computer, what kind of software they plan to use, what applications will be done on the computer, and so on. They may talk about the need for speed or reliability, but unless the salesperson probes further, customers generally won't offer their deeper reasons for wanting certain product attributes.

Suppose Marilyn's customer says he wants a computer that is easy to use. He is not likely to tell her the reason: he is embarrassed because of his computer illiteracy, and he wants a product that will make him look good despite his lack of computer savvy. A skillful customer-focused rep such as Marilyn will gently probe until she discovers the true reason that ease of use is important.

Why does this matter? Unless Marilyn understands her customer's need to look good, she may offer him a product that is more difficult to use but otherwise an excellent value. But she will never get the sale, because this product will fail to address one of the customer's most important motivations: to look good in front of his peers.

Here's another example. Suppose a salesperson is trying to sell a car to a customer who has just walked onto the dealer's lot. The customer says he is looking for a mid-size car with a V-6 engine, AM/FM stereo cassette, power door and window features, and a lease package.

This seems like a specific set of requirements, enough for the salesperson to begin recommending certain cars to the customer. But the salesperson is missing the most important information he needs to know: what the customer *really* wants is an expensive car that will impress his friends. He doesn't have much cash for a down payment, but he could afford a lease if it didn't require any money down. As for the AM/FM stereo cassette, he doesn't care much if it has one or not; he never listens to music in the car. He only said he wanted the radio and tape player in response to the salesperson's canned question about features.

Unless the salesperson probed for this information, it's easy to see how he or she could show the customer a dozen cars that fit his surface needs without presenting him with one car that passes the most important test of looking impressive to his friends.

One more example from my own experience: I once visited a chemical producer who was interested in purchasing a new scientific instrument system that checked the quality of the customer's final product. As the customer and I were talking about his needs, I asked about the recent changes in his department. He stated emotionally that his staff had been cut by more than 75 percent and that he now had to operate three additional instruments. He didn't know how he would be able to learn and remember the operation of these three different products.

Once I understood his deeper need for a system that was easy to learn and remember, I was in a better position to satisfy him. I went back to my company, and we ended up customizing the user interface of our product so that it would match that of a product the customer was currently using, one that was familiar to him.

Surface needs are learned by both types of salespeople during the qualification step. Internal needs are discovered only by customer-focused salespeople.

By searching for customers' deeper needs, customer-focused salespeople achieve two major advantages:

1. They differentiate themselves from their competitors who do not strive to find out customers' deeper needs. Customer-focused reps are viewed by customers, not as "just another salesperson" but as people who genuinely want to help. As a result, they quickly gain their customers' trust.

2. They gather valuable information that helps to ensure they will be able to satisfy the customer at a deep level, which in turn helps to ensure that the customer will buy again.

During this step, Marilyn also probes to find out how the customer has gone about making purchase decisions in the past. When it comes to buying patterns, history usually repeats itself. If the customer always makes a point of reading the brochures of six companies before deciding to buy, he will probably do the same thing this time. Marilyn won't try to dissuade him from doing so.

In asking the customer to describe how past buying decisions were made, Marilyn also asks about past decisions the customer made that he would have changed if he had to do it over again. In this way, she can help the customer to avoid making the same mistakes again.

This information is particularly important if the regret was caused by an action of the salesperson, e.g., if a customer bought a computer because he was pressured into buying by the salesperson before he had sufficient time to look at competitive products. In that case, he may regret the decision even if he's happy with the product.

Here are some examples of questions Marilyn might ask to determine how the customer has made buying decisions in the past:

- Thinking back to your previous purchase, can you describe the sequence of events that led up to the decision to buy?
- Which sales rep did the best job of meeting your needs and expectations? In what way?
- What are some of the things the salespeople did that helped you to make the purchase decision?
- What did the salespeople do that hindered your decision?
- What similarities or differences do you see between this purchase and your last purchase?
- What can I do to help you evaluate my product and make sure you are satisfied with whatever purchase decision you make?

Step 3: Presenting Information

Sales-Driven. Once Don has qualified his customer, he begins to shower him with information, starting with a product brochure that's filled with technical information about the product's characteristics and specifications. Don hasn't bothered to highlight any information for the customer; he feels that everything is equally important and the more information he gives the customer, the better.

This is the typical approach of the sales-driven sales rep: to bombard the customer with any and all information about the product and the company. The theory is that the more information a salesperson gives to a customer, the more impressed the customer will be. In truth, more information usually means more confusion for the customer.

I remember when one of my salespeople came into my office with a hefty sales proposal that contained twenty pages of product features. I leafed through the proposal, searching for the part that discussed the customer's needs. There wasn't one. When I asked the rep how he expected the customer to read and understand the proposal, he responded, "I spent more than two hours personally reviewing the proposal with him." I can only imagine how the poor customer felt after that session. This salesperson had failed to consider the customer's needs; instead, he was more interested in showing off all that he knew. The buying process was delayed so long by the complicated proposal that the customer eventually lost its budget for the project to another department.

Being a typical sales-driven rep, Don also likes to brag about his product knowledge. In addition to giving his customer a stack of brochures, product spec sheets, advertisements, annual reports, and whatever else he can find in his office, Don bombards the customer with verbal information about the product, including some of the things he just learned in a product seminar.

Don never pauses to see how or whether the customer is digesting this information. He just keeps rattling off the facts he knows about the product's features. One reason he focuses on features is that it's hard for him to zero in on benefits that might be of interest to the customer, since he didn't spend much time probing to find out what the customer really wants. For instance, he never bothered to find out that the customer feels extremely uncomfortable with technology and as a result hardly understands a word that Don is saying right now.

Customer-Focused. Before she presents any information, Marilyn asks the customer how he wants his information presented. Does he learn best by seeing a sales proposal, listening to a presentation, participating in a product demo, or by some other means?

People have widely varying preferences for how they want information communicated to them and the level of detail they desire. Some want a minimum of information, some want every detail before they are ready to make a purchase decision. The customer-focused rep finds out these preferences before presenting any information. The sales-driven rep never asks.

One successful salesman I know always lets his customers guide him in presenting information. For example, one customer told him "I'm a direct type of person, so make your presentation 'to the point.' " He did, developing a tailored presentation that not only won him the immediate order but helped him to establish a successful long-term relationship with the customer.

If the salesperson doesn't ask, customers may not say how they want information presented. But they'll resent the salesperson who gives them information in a way that doesn't work for them.

When a customer asks for information about the product, the customer-focused rep probes further rather than rattling off a list of features. And unlike sales-driven reps, customer-focused salespeople don't bombard customers with information. Instead, they carefully select the information to present to customers, based on an understanding of their surface and deeper needs.

Before her visit, Marilyn had already sent a product brochure on which she had highlighted the information she thought would be relevant to the customer. On the back of a business card attached to the brochure, she'd written a brief note: "Jack, I went through and highlighted information that I thought may interest you."

Now, during her face-to-face sales call, she reviews the highlighted portions of the brochure with the customer, explains technical buzzwords, and talks about the differences in terminology used by different vendors, so that the customer will be able to compare her product information with that of a competitor. (If the product literature is filled with buzzwords, Marilyn will make up a brief glossary of terms and send that to the customer as well.)

While Marilyn is presenting information about her product, the customer is not only attempting to understand what she's saying but to differentiate her product from the competition's. Marilyn knows this, so she makes a point of focusing on the unique capabilities of her product that are relevant to the customer.

The key words are "unique" and "relevant." It's not enough to present product benefits to a customer. The benefits have to be relevant to the customer. If one benefit of a particular computer is ease of use, this may be highly relevant to a computer novice but irrelevant to someone who is a computer whiz. The customer-focused salesperson presents only those capabilities that the customer will view as beneficial.

Even this is not enough. The customer also wants to know why he or she should buy one company's product over another's. So the customer-focused salesperson stresses not just a product's benefits, but its advantages over the competition. An advantage is simply a benefit the competition doesn't offer.

For example, in the specialty chemical business, one of the

customer's most important needs is for safety. Suppose that ABC Chemical Company provides a particular scale inhibitor (a chemical that prevents the formation of hard mineral salts that can block water lines) in a dry powder form that comes in a bag. The operator must tear open the bag and dump its contents into a mixing tank.

XYZ Company provides the same scale inhibitor in a disposable liquid bin with its own pump and feed system. There is no handling required, so workers are never exposed to the harmful chemicals inside. This is not just a benefit but a key advantage over ABC's product.

An advantage that addresses a customer's deeper needs is an even more powerful selling point. Let's go back to the example of Karen Johnson, whose story opened the chapter. The salesperson who did enough probing would find out that the person who previously held Karen's position was fired because the computer system went down during a crucial marketing campaign and the vendor didn't address the problem for two days. Karen is worried about losing her job if something similar happens with a new system.

Suppose one vendor offers 24-hour-a-day service, or a backup system that no competitor offers. This advantage would be highly relevant to Karen, since it would address a deep concern—her fear of being fired. Other things being equal, the vendor that offers the best service package is likely to win Karen's business.

Not only should the information presented be relevant to customer needs, but even the artwork on the product literature should be relevant to customers, as Marilyn discovered with another customer. Her company lost a contract for an engineering firm. One reason, Marilyn learned later, was that the winner's product appeared more field-ready, because the product brochure showed an operator with a hard hat. Marilyn's brochure had a picture of a user in a pristine office environment.

The message is to make certain that your product literature is consistent with the needs and expectations of the customer. This may require that the sales department work more closely with the marketing department to develop customer-focused brochures.

Step 4: Handling Objections

Sales-Driven. When a customer raises an objection, it indicates that he or she feels ambivalent about buying a product. The most common objections are no need, no money, no hurry, and no confidence in the salesperson and/or the salesperson's company.

Don tries to overcome objections in one of two ways: by presenting additional information, or by minimizing the objections by restating all of the positive attributes of the product.

In this case, the prospect (an office manager) has told Don that he doesn't need the new telephone system Don is trying to sell him. Following is an excerpt from an exchange between Don and the customer:

Office manager: I don't need a new telephone system. Our current system does the few things we need it to do.

Don: That's exactly why you should buy a new phone system. The reason you only do a few things with your ten-year-old system is because it doesn't have all of the latest features you could be using. [Don goes on to explain all the new features.]

When Don's customers say they're in no hurry to purchase a new product, Don immediately thinks that they have an ulterior motive—for example, maybe they're talking to a competitor. Instead of accepting the customers' objections at face value, Don attempts to pressure them into buying by minimizing their objections and getting them to focus on all of the benefits of the product.

Here's how a sales-driven rep like Don would try to force an unwanted investment product on a customer—in this case, a retired banker who made it clear he was in no hurry to buy the products the rep was trying to sell him.

Customer: Let me think about it.

Rep: I can understand your wanting to think this decision over. I'd like to ask you a couple of questions. Which of these two investments best meets your needs, the index mutual fund or the bond fund?

Customer: The index mutual fund.

Rep: What about the index mutual fund did you like?

Customer: [*Describes the specific things he likes about the fund.*]

Rep: With all of those positives, why not let your money start working for you right now?

After this conversation has ended, the banker is angry because he knows that the salesperson tried to manipulate him into buying. The fact that the rep used the retiree's own words to try and pressure him to buy only adds to his anger.

In both examples, the customer's objections are overridden by the forceful responses of the sales-driven rep. This manipulative style of handling objections alienates customers and makes it less likely that they will buy.

My friend Jenny provides a good example of this. Jenny was shopping for a laptop computer. She called a number of mail-order firms trying to find the make and model she wanted. One of the people she talked to was an aggressive, sales-driven rep. My friend told him what she wanted—a Toshiba model, because she had a strong preference for its keyboard and screen. The salesman said he didn't have the model she wanted in stock, but he told her about another laptop he could sell her that was a much better deal. Jenny wasn't familiar with the brand, but it *did* sound like a great deal. She told the rep that she wanted to find the product in a local store and check out the keyboard and screen before deciding whether to buy it. If she liked the product, she would call him back that day to order it.

But the salesperson ignored her objection and pressured her to place her order immediately. He reiterated all of the positive features of the product and stressed the terrific package price. He told her she could send it back if she didn't like it. He kept insisting that she buy right away. Not only did she not buy, she didn't bother to check out the computer in a local store. Had the salesperson been more low key, taken her objections seriously, and let her overcome them herself, he might have made the sale. Instead, Jenny decided that she'd rather pay more for a machine than buy one at a great price from this obnoxious salesperson.

Customer-Focused. The customer-focused rep handles objections in an entirely different way. The customer-focused approach is to prevent objections from arising in the first place by doing a good job of qualifying and uncovering needs, the first two steps of the selling process.

By carefully identifying surface and deeper needs and establishing budget limits, Marilyn discovers early in the selling process whether or not there is the potential for a sale. If there is clearly no potential, she ends the process. Not so the sales-driven rep, who does a poor job of qualifying and uncovering needs and may try to make the sale even if there is no apparent customer need for the product.

Another way that customer-focused salespeople like Marilyn prevent objections is by discussing the limitations of their products. This minimizes the "no confidence" objection.

The sales-driven sales rep would never dream of presenting the limitations of a product along with its advantages. Their reasoning is: "Why ruin the chance of getting the order by talking about the negative aspects of a product?"

There are two good reasons. The first, mentioned above, is that being honest will strengthen the level of trust between the salesperson and the customer. Every product has some weakness, and if the salesperson doesn't mention them, the customer will naturally wonder whether the rep is hiding something.

Which brings up the next reason for candor: If the rep doesn't tell customers about product limitations, you can bet that competitors will. And what they say may be a distortion of the truth.

In bringing up limitations, if there are any that can be overcome by other products or options, Marilyn lets the customer know this. And if there is a limitation that cannot be overcome, she is honest about it—even if it means losing the sale to a competitor. This sale may be lost, but the customer will remember how fairly he was treated and will likely buy from Marilyn in the future. Remember, the customer-focused salesperson is interested in developing relationships, not making fast commissions.

No matter how carefully the customer-focused salesperson qualifies customers and uncovers their needs, there is the possibility that some objections will arise later in the selling process. If objections do arise, the customer-focused salesperson doesn't try to overcome or minimize them, as the sales-driven rep would. Instead, the rep helps customers to resolve the objections themselves. This further strengthens the bond of trust between them.

Suppose the customer comes back with a common objection: "Your product is too expensive." Here is how Marilyn would help the customer to handle the objection. She would:

- Thank the customer for being open and honest about the objection.
- Not defend her high price or come back with a discount.
- Ask the customer how being higher priced rates her product relative to its competitors, in terms of the cost-benefit ratio. Even if her product costs more than a competitor's, it may have advantages that justify the higher price.
  For example, it may be that the customer is looking for fast response and excellent service as well as low cost. If Marilyn's product costs $5,000 more than the competition's, but her company's fast response to problems will save the customer more than $5,000 in lost productivity the first time a service call is needed, the higher price is justified.
- Find out the implications to the customer of choosing her higher priced product. For example, would the customer be in danger of losing his job?
  If the implications are serious (e.g., the customer may lose his job if he doesn't recommend a low-cost product), she will ask the customer: "Will it be worth your time and mine to look for ways to bring the price down to an acceptable level?" This is a crucial question. If the customer is not committed to her product, Marilyn knows it makes no sense to look for ways of reducing the price.

By probing in this way, Marilyn is helping the customer review his concerns about her offering. If, after reviewing the cost-benefit ratio of her product versus competitive offerings, the customer decides hers is the product he prefers, then Marilyn can begin to work out an acceptable price. One way to reduce the price is to eliminate an option that is relatively unimportant to the customer. Another possibility is to offer the customer more liberal payment options.

Sometimes these questions bring up an issue that the salesperson overlooked earlier and that may be a source of the customer's ambivalence about buying. For example, the customer might tell the rep about a strong feature of a competitor's offering that doesn't seem to meet a current need. By going back to Step 2 and probing further, the sales rep may discover that the competitor's product meets a future need that the rep failed to uncover. If so, the rep may be able to come up with another product or option that will match the competitor's product advantage.

By taking the time to help the customer review their products objectively, customer-focused salespeople stand out from their competitors. And because the customer makes the buying decision rather than being pressured into it by the salesperson, there is less likelihood that the customer will regret the purchase.

Step 5: Closing

Sales-Driven. Once Don goes beyond the presentation stage and the handling (or ignoring) of objections, he "comes in for the kill." As soon as the customer shows any signs of making a decision, Don takes over and uses one or more manipulative techniques to try and close the sale.

One of his favorites is the Ben Franklin close. This manipulative close seems to give control over the final purchase decision to the customer. Here's how it works: Don draws a T on a blank page. He then proceeds to ask the customer to list all the reasons why she doesn't want to buy, and he writes these on one side of the T. Then he asks her to list all of the positive aspects of the product that would make her want to buy it. He keeps asking questions until the *pro* side of the T is longer than the *con* side. Then he pressures the customer into giving him the order by showing that the positives outweigh the negatives.

Other sales-driven closes are less subtle than the Ben Franklin technique. For example, the assumptive close presumes the person is going to buy, even though the customer hasn't yet made the decision. Don will say something like, "By the way, when would you like the product delivered?" before the customer has indicated an intention to buy.

A more subtle, equally manipulative variation of the assumptive close is to turn a customer's question into a purchase decision. When the customer asks, "Does your product come with a laser printer?" Don makes a note on a blank purchase order while turning the question into a statement: "So you would like this product to include a laser printer." If the customer says nothing, the next step is to get the purchase order number.

The rule of thumb for the sales-driven salesperson is never to give up on closing until the customer says no seven times or throws the sales rep out of his office. This is part of the reason that sales-driven salespeople have developed so many different closing techniques. If the customer says no to one technique, the rep simply tries another tactic.

Some sales trainers suggest that this approach is more effective on smaller purchases that involve little financial risk. This may be true, but it's beside the point. Even if aggressive closes help the salesperson to land the order, they ensure that the customer will never again buy a product from that person. No one likes to be pressured into making any type of decision.

Customer-Focused. Marilyn doesn't use any techniques to close the sale. There is no "close" under the customer-focused approach. The customer simply decides to buy or not to buy, based on all of the previous steps in the process. Whether or not the customer chooses to buy depends on how effectively the rep resolved the customer's concerns, provided relevant information, and gained smaller scale commitments. But the final decision is out of the salesperson's hands.

Many salespeople feel threatened by the approach of letting the customer make the final decision, but, ironically, it's the best way to win the order. One plant manager of a Fortune 100 company told Brent, a customer-focused salesperson, that everyone at the plant agreed he was the most effective of all of the reps who contacted them. The reason, the manager told Brent, is that "you don't tell us how to make our decisions, like the other sales reps do." The lesson to be learned: to get control requires giving up control to the customer.

Customer-Focused Selling: Model of the Future

The sales-driven salesperson is a product of the same mentality that focuses on short-term profits at the expense of long-term growth. Sales-driven reps will do anything to win in the short term. In contrast, the customer-focused salesperson strives to develop a long-term relationship with the customer, one that will lead to many sales in the future.

The sales-driven salesperson can still succeed where competition is limited. But as competition intensifies and customers demand higher quality, customer-focused selling is quickly becoming the only viable approach to achieving long-term success. Those salespeople who continue to use manipulative techniques to make the sale will increasingly lose out to their customer-focused competitors.

It's not easy to make the switch from a sales-driven orientation to a customer-focused approach. But with time, training, reward, and the full commitment of the sales manager, the transformation to a customer-focused selling approach can be made. The results, in terms of customer satisfaction, enhanced reputation, and long-term relationships, will make the effort worthwhile.

Note

1. Sandra Millers Young, "Sales Savvy for the Nineties," *Training and Development*, December 1992: 13.

Chapter 8

The 120-Day Plan

Many sales managers take on new assignments without doing any planning. Even veteran managers rush into field sales management positions with the goal of immediately solving all of the problems in their district or region, from low productivity to high expenses. They spend their first weeks or months on the job judging their performance on the basis of the number of problems they "fix." Some of them panic when they find that the same problems keep recurring. When one fire is put out, another fire is sparked somewhere else in the territory. Soon all of their time is spent in reacting to crises.

Because they are reacting to problems rather than planning to prevent them, sales continue to decline and expenses to rise. With every day, they feel less in control of the situation. Soon they feel pressure from senior management to show results. They put poor performing salespeople on probation and work even harder and faster to put out fires, but it's a losing battle.

This scenario is a familiar one. Too many sales managers fall into the trap of reacting to events instead of planning strategy. Because they do not set up a deliberate game plan for their first few months in the job, their ships and crews (the sales force) drift aimlessly in whatever direction the wind and currents take them.

You only get one chance to make a first impression. Whether you are a rookie sales manager or a seasoned veteran, if you don't take charge in the first 120 days on the job, it will take at least another 120 days to win the support of your salespeople and your manager. A superstar sales team may help to cover up a weak startup period. But eventually, your lack of leadership will show through. That's why it's vital to have a specific plan of action for the first 30, 60, 90, and 120 days in your new sales management assignment.

The First Thirty Days

There are three things you should do in your first thirty days[1] on the job: travel with your salespeople, involve them, and set your expectations. To do more or less during the first thirty days will either overwhelm salespeople or cause them to view you as a weak leader.

Traveling With Reps

Traveling with salespeople is a major first step toward building trust. Have you ever heard the sales manager's office described as a tomb? It's an apt analogy. Nothing crucial ever happens in the office; it happens in the car and in face-to-face meetings with customers. Get out of the office and travel with your people as soon as you can.

Upper management may ask you to explain the purpose of traveling with your reps. Your salespeople may also question your purpose. Tell both groups that the only way you can accurately appraise sales performance is by observing salespeople in action.

You may find that some salespeople are insecure about having you tag along. Ask them why. Is their self-confidence low? Are they questioning your motives? The sooner you can find out their concerns, the sooner you can address them. And these concerns must be addressed; otherwise, a communication barrier will begin to build and trust will be lost.

Before traveling with your salespeople, let them know when and why you will participate during a sales call. Your primary role during the call is that of observer. You want to see how your reps perform so that you can coach them after the call and help them to improve their skills. However, it's good for you to participate in the call, at least to a small extent; you don't want to stand in the corner of the customer's office like a potted plant.

When to jump in during a face-to-face sales call is a dilemma for many new and experienced managers. If the visit is to an account that's projected to close within the next ninety days, you should participate where necessary to help your salesperson win the customer's commitment. If the sale is longer term than ninety days, spend most of your time observing rather than participating.

While observing, don't take notes. Doing so may fluster the salesperson and annoy or distract the customer. And there's no need for notes; after you go on a few calls, you will see the salesperson repeat the same behaviors and responses, good and bad.

Coaching

It's a good idea to go on several sales calls before coaching your salespeople. Even though your reps may pressure you to give them instant feedback, let them know that you have some observations to make, but you want them to be accurate, so it's best to see them in action in other calls.

In rare cases, immediate feedback is necessary. For instance, if your salesperson is one hour late for his first call and doesn't call the customer to let her know, this disrespectful behavior must be brought to the rep's attention immediately.

When you start coaching, after the first few calls, focus on salespeople's strengths. If you acknowledge their strengths first, they will pay more attention to your ideas about how to improve areas of weakness. And if you show them how they can make improvements without changing their basic selling style, they will be even more receptive to what you have to say.

Suppose a salesperson has what I call an expressive style of selling. By "expressive," I mean that the salesperson is an effective socializer who wins sales primarily by relationship-building. This is positive, but in my experience such reps often fail to plan adequately before sales calls, so they don't get all the information they need and have to make an extra call or two to fill the gap.

To help this type of rep to develop planning skills, the sales manager should focus on the rep's strength in the area of relationship-building. Following is an example of how this can be done. The dialogue is between Phil, who has an expressive selling style, and his sales manager, who is coaching him in the skill of planning. This conversation takes place after the sales manager has spent two days with Phil, joining him in six face-to-face sales calls.

Sales manager: Phil, you selected a good mix of accounts for us to visit—key accounts, customers needing further support, and immediate sales situations.

Phil: That's the way I like to plan your trips down here. I realize you are quite busy, so I want to give you a good idea of what's happening when I do have you in my territory.

Sales manager: One of the things I am quite pleased with is how you build relationships with your customers. What else do you think you can do to build upon your selling skills?

Phil: Probably know the new products better than I currently do.

Sales manager: I know you'll pick up on those new products quickly. I'm thinking more in terms of selling skills.

Phil: I don't know. What do you think?

Sales manager: It seems that we went into many of these calls with some good precall objectives, such as finding out who will be on the customer's evaluation team. But we may have been able to discover more information.

Phil: What do you mean?

Sales manager: By planning a set group of questions prior to the calls, we could have walked out with information on how the customer views the competition and how the buying process will proceed. We can build on your excellent people skills to get your customers to talk more about these two important issues. You're an experienced rep, and I certainly don't expect you to write a list of questions before every call. But you might try guiding the conversation in the areas where you need information. And to do that, you have to plan ahead, to think about the specific information you want to gather. (Pause). What do you think?

Phil: Yeah . . . I see.

Sales manager: Why do you think it's important to practice covering these two areas during your sales call?

Phil: Well, if you know the customer's internal needs and buying process, you definitely have a better handle on the account.

Sales manager: That's true, and there's something more. Being part of a quality organization means doing things right the first time. While you take three to four sales calls to get all the information you need, there is a competitor getting that same information in one sales call. While you are still in the information collection stage on your third sales call at an account, your competitor is ready to close.

Phil: That's a good point.

Sales manager: The next sales call at three o'clock is a long-term prospect that won't place an order for the next two to three years, right?

Phil: Yes.

Sales manager: Why don't I show you how to gather more information from this customer, using your own selling style. You can open the call and do your best to accomplish the precall objectives. Let's plan ahead what information we want to gather. At the end of the call, if you still need more information, I'll show you how to guide the customer to talk more about his internal needs and the buying process, using your own conversational style. Then we'll have you attempt to follow my example in tomorrow's calls. How's that for a plan?

Phil: Let's do it.

Sales manager: Before we work together in this area, do you have any concerns?

Phil: Just one. Although this approach sounds good, sometimes you can't have each sales call go the way you want. Each sales call is different.

Sales manager: That's right, but you can have *most* calls go your way if you spend just a little time planning before the call. Suppose you were working on ten different sales situations simultaneously, and you made one sales call to each account in one week without attempting to plan before each sales call. You'd have to have made at least one more call to each account to gather the additional information you need. That means you would need an extra week to get the information needed. Now, if you planned before each call, chances are you may still have to make another call to get more information on some of the accounts, but you won't have to visit all ten. Let's say you'll save three business days by planning your calls and guiding the conversation. Is that enough of a savings to justify planning before each call?

Phil: I never thought of it that way.

After this dialogue, it's important to follow up with Phil. On returning to the office, the sales manager should send a letter to Phil that reinforces his selling strengths in the area of relationship-building and encourages him to work on planning. This should be followed up by a phone call to get Phil's feedback and answer any questions he might have.

Following is a list of simple steps to follow when coaching salespeople:

1. Recognize and praise the salesperson's strengths (in the case above, excellent people skills).
2. Get salespeople involved; ask them what they believe are areas that need improving.
3. Tell them what skill you think needs improving and explain the importance of the skill by showing how it impacts their ability to make the sale.
4. Get the salesperson's agreement on the need for improvement.
5. Develop a plan for improvement.
6. Resolve concerns and overcome resistance.
7. Follow up with a trip report emphasizing the skill that needs developing.
8. After sending the trip report, phone the salesperson to discuss any remaining concerns.
9. Watch for improvement in future calls.

Establishing Trust and Credibility

For your coaching message to have the maximum impact, there must be an environment of trust between you and your salespeople. Trust comes from being open with your sales reps and showing a genuine concern for their success.

Trust is established in part through open communications. I know one sales manager who didn't take the trouble to state explicitly why he was making quarterly visits to one of his salespeople's territories. Previous managers never used to travel with this salesperson, so the rep thought that if the sales manager didn't visit, this signaled that he was doing a good job.

After nine months of tension and suspicion, the salesperson finally asked his new manager why he kept coming to his territory. Once the manager explained his purpose (to do some coaching), the tension disappeared.

The sales manager could have prevented the rep's anxiety by telling him from the start why he was visiting. Nine months is a long time to wait to establish a trusting relationship.

Another way to prevent tension and mistrust is by learning something about your salespeople before you travel with them. Look through their personnel files. The files will not only include salary history, resumes, and job applications, but should also contain previous performance appraisals. By studying these appraisals, you'll be able to learn something about your reps' strengths and weaknesses before you see them in action.

Although you'll certainly want to review your predecessor's comments about your sales team, don't take those comments as gospel. When I took on a sales manager's job for the first time, my predecessor's assessment of one new salesperson suggested that he wasn't making enough sales calls. That turned out not to be the case. During his first six months, that rookie salesperson went door-to-door to build up a sales pipeline. Just looking at the salesperson's current pipeline activity told me that my predecessor had overlooked a positive new hire behavior.

Take the time to let salespeople give their views of a previous manager's comments. This will send a positive, motivating signal to your reps that you trust them, that you are not coming to the job with any preconceived notions about their performance and capabilities.

Whenever there is a change in management, salespeople expect things will be different. You can use this expectation to establish a positive environment from the start. Ask your salespeople what hinders their performance the most. You may be surprised to learn that you're the first manager to show that much concern.

Your credibility and the level of trust you establish with salespeople will depend on how, and how soon, you respond to their concerns and frustrations. You won't be able to address every one of them immediately, but do what you can, as soon as you can, in order to build a solid base of support.

There is one caveat to remember when responding to salespeople's concerns: only respond to the problems of your direct reports. If you are a national sales manager, with district managers reporting to you, you can listen to their salespeople's concerns, but have them work through their own managers, not you, to resolve them. Otherwise, you undermine the authority of your direct reports.

As part of your effort to create a positive environment, have your assistant ask each salesperson for his or her birthday and wedding anniversary date, if the rep is married. Log these dates on your calendar and make a point of acknowledging them in an appropriate way. For example, during one of my trips to his territory, a salesperson mentioned that he likes peanut butter sandwiches. Later in the month, he traveled with his wife to New Orleans on an anniversary trip. Through casual conversation, I found out where he was staying. When he and his wife walked into their hotel room, there was a lovely gift basket of fruits and cheeses waiting for them, and a peanut butter sandwich on the side. This small gesture made a big impression and helped to reinforce a positive working relationship.

One-on-One Meetings

Sit down with each salesperson after you've had a chance to travel with him or her. The goal of these one-on-one meetings is to get the salesperson involved in your team. It's often valuable to have an unbiased third party—a previous manager, a senior salesperson, or perhaps someone from human resources—meet with your salespeople to solicit their anonymous feedback before these one-on-one meetings, then report to you the concerns that were brought up (again, maintaining anonymity). In this way, you will gain valuable information that salespeople may not have divulged to you directly.

It's important to be yourself at these meetings, but it's equally important to be professional. Don't get too chummy; you want to be viewed and respected as a manager, not a buddy.

It's best to hold these meetings in the office. Never conduct a meeting in a bar over drinks, or your sales reps may think that you want to use cocktails as a truth serum to get them to reveal things they'd rather not.

Wherever you hold your meeting, here are some of the questions to ask your salespeople: What are the strengths and weaknesses of the district? What opportunities should we take advantage of? Are your goals and priorities clear? What do you, as the new manager, need to know that you don't already know? What requires immediate attention? What does the rep already know about you?

Group Meetings

Look for patterns among your salespeople's responses to these questions. Perhaps you can make addressing these concerns one of the objectives of your first group meeting with the sales force. That accomplishes two things: It shows your interest in salespeople's concerns, and it suggests that their involvement in the management process is important to you.

Some managers argue that giving salespeople the chance to talk about their concerns only invites them to conduct a gripe session. But in my experience, if you handle them well, these meetings yield positive, not negative, results.

Take the chance with your first sales meeting. Set up an agenda that allows your salespeople to control 50 percent of the meeting, but make them stick to the agenda.

One effective approach is to give each salesperson three questions they'll have to answer in ten minutes during the group meeting. For example, during a period of major change in corporate structure, I held a group meeting and asked each salesperson to answer these questions: How have these changes affected you?

How have you handled these changes? What's your vision of future possibilities for you, your territory, and the company?

One by one, the salespeople reflected on all the company changes in the course of their ten-minute presentations. Their overwhelming concern was to keep their minds focused on their territories and not to let rumors, or changes happening elsewhere in the company, affect their performance. Far from deteriorating into a gripe session, this meeting was extremely upbeat, and it reinforced the salespeople's determination to forge ahead in the midst of uncertainty.

To build trust, make sure that *your* attitude is positive. I know of one new sales manager who set a negative tone for his first meeting with his salespeople by displaying on an overhead transparency a list of things that angered him the most. The message that came across was: "You're here to please me." He obviously wanted salespeople to leave the meeting thinking: "I'd better not do these things if I want to remain on my manager's good side." He never listened to what his people had to say, or to what they needed from him in order to improve their performance. Needless to say, his salespeople didn't trust him. Morale was low and backbiting was common in his district. The moral? If you want to establish a positive working environment, start with yourself.

Setting Expectations

Take the time to explain your management philosophy to your salespeople. Sales reps want to know how you will be evaluating their performance.

Let your salespeople know there is more to succeeding than achieving quotas. Tell them you will be evaluating them on three aspects of their sales performance: (1) sales numbers, (2) goals, and (3) customer-focused behaviors that lead to sales numbers. Stress your desire to see continuous improvement, and let your reps know you will give them frequent feedback and reward specific accomplishments and behaviors.

Now is the time to introduce your salespeople to the Progressive Goal Management system outlined in Chapter 3. Let your people know that by pursuing goals, they will soon notice improvements in terms of territory development and self-development. Then, tell them that you expect them to be setting goals by the start of the next quarter.

After you discuss goal-setting, explain the importance of making quality an integral part of the sales process. Give a brief overview of the process of customer-focused selling, as described in Chapter 7. Let your reps know which customer-focused behaviors or performance factors will be graded in their performance reviews (see Chapter 6 on measurement and feedback).

You can get a head start on improving these behaviors at your first group meeting by having your reps make team presentations that focus on using these different skills. For example, one team could present its approach to territory development, and another might cover examples of communication skills they've used. The idea is to get all of your salespeople involved in making your performance expectations clear.

Unfortunately, no matter how good the presentations or the materials you hand out at the meeting, once some salespeople get back to their territories, your good efforts will be lost in space. To bring them back to earth, distribute or post your expectations, as well as top management's values and expectations, in a prominent place as a constant reminder.

Reinforce your own expectations during one-on-one travel with salespeople. And don't be afraid to repeat yourself—frequently if necessary.

If one of your salespeople isn't covering the territory well, give specific examples of good territory management. Refer that salesperson to your written description of effective territory management (if you don't have one, write one now). The habits you develop at the start of your assignment will set the tone for the rest of the year.

Set up some type of performance log for your salespeople, so that you can begin to monitor their progress over the course of the year. The log can be informal. After reviewing with your reps the performance factors on which they will be graded at year-end (see Chapter 3), simply jot down in a notebook each week how they are performing in each of the areas. Even better, consider developing a computer-based system so that you can enter a running log that shows how salespeople are meeting or falling short of expectations.

Share your log with your salespeople periodically, so they have a written record of their performance, which they can refer to on a regular basis. This action will reinforce the concept of continuous improvement.

Make sure you give your salespeople plenty of feedback. As noted in Chapter 3, inadequate feedback is a common shortcoming of many sales managers. For example, I know one sales manager who would evaluate his salespeople on the basis of their "concern for cost and profits" without explaining what he meant by these terms and without giving his salespeople any specific feedback in this area. One day, one of his salespeople received a letter from the manager that read "Your turning in expense reports late lowers our profitability." In his performance review, the rep received a substandard rating, partly because of this. The salesperson was shocked. He'd had no prior feedback and no idea of the connection between late expense reports and profitability. The moral: Set your expectations early, make them clear, and provide frequent feedback.

The First Sixty Days

During the first thirty days, you traveled with and coached your salespeople, opened the doors to communication, and set your expectations. Now, you are ready to move on to crucial territorial problems and administrative matters.

Addressing Poor Performers

Being responsible for a sales operation means bringing immediate sales dollars to your organization. And that means you must be prepared to terminate those salespeople who aren't living up to expectations.

Now is the time to give your poor performers written interim appraisals, in which you objectively review the level of their productivity since you came onboard. These written appraisals should be reinforced with informal one-on-one discussions and feedback.

In addition to addressing known poor performers, target those territories that appear to be problems and learn everything you can about them. Try to determine whether the economic conditions or the salesperson's skills are the root cause of unacceptable sales performance. If the problem is with the salesperson, take time out to coach him or her in order to improve performance.

In some cases, all the salesperson needs is to have his or her confidence boosted. For example, a new sales rep named Steve, who worked for my colleague Chuck, inherited a problem territory when he joined the firm, which sells computer systems. Steve claimed his quota was $300,000 too high, and he confided that he had little confidence he would achieve it.

Instead of lowering Steve's quota, Chuck subscribed to the Sunday edition of the local newspaper in this problem territory, so that he could follow the progress of new businesses in the area. By looking in the classified section at the ads of businesses that were likely prospects for Steve's products, Chuck was able to identify which companies were expanding and might represent the best potential for future sales.

Then he passed this information on to Steve. He never told Steve where he got the information, because he didn't want him to believe he was looking over his shoulder. When Steve asked Chuck how he heard of these expansions, Chuck said he had heard it through his network.

As Chuck continued to provide leads over the next several months, he noticed that Steve gradually began to discard his self-limiting beliefs of having too high a quota. In time, Steve became a consistent million-dollar producer.

Territory Presentations

In addition to targeting problem territories, ask all salespeople to prepare presentations describing the problems and opportunities in their territories. The intent is for you to understand the perspective of your salespeople and for them to learn by going through the process of developing a presentation. Following are examples of the type and level of questions your salespeople should address in their presentations. In this case, the salespeople are marketing scientific equipment to government, university, and corporate accounts.

Market Segmentation

- What percentage of your total account base is government? university? industrial?

- Of government business, what percentage is:
  —defense-related?
  —regulatory?
  —forensic?
  —other?
- Of university business, what percentage is:
  —large universities?
  —small teaching schools?
- Of industrial business, what percentage is petrochemical, polymer, semiconductor, etc. (use SIC codes to segment business).

Applications

- What are the major product applications in each segment? In the entire territory?

Competition

- Who are your competitors' key accounts?
- On which accounts do you feel our company can do a better job than the competition?
- How do these key accounts network with other accounts and key contacts?
- Who are the competitor salespeople in your territory?
- Where do you encounter them most frequently? Least frequently? Where are their offices? Support staff?
- What is the estimated share of market that each competitor owns in your territory?

Pipeline

- What percentage of market share of your territory do you own?
- What is the total sales potential in the territory?
- What is your won/lost ratio?
- What is the source of most of your leads—advertising? referrals? trade shows? another source?
- Roughly how many of each type of lead do you generate each month?

- How many suspects, long-term prospects, and solid orders do you need in your pipeline to make your monthly sales number?
- What are your prospecting plans? Are there any professional/industry group meetings that offer networking opportunities in your territory? Where are the key networks of companies, professional societies, scientists, and engineers located?
- Do these networks represent business potential? If they do, what are you doing to maximize your exposure to these groups?

Territory Management

- What are the different pockets of business in your geographic territory?
- Is the time you spend in each pocket proportional to the sales potential in each pocket?
- Is the number of prospects in your prospecting system proportional to the sales potential in each of your geographic pockets?
- Considering the mix of business in your territory, what two actions would increase sales by $100,000 or more over the next year?

Before your reps make their presentations, do some homework of your own. Select a commercial database that most closely resembles your customer profile. Compare the profile of customers from the database with the information reported by your salespeople in their presentations. Be prepared to question them about any obvious discrepancies. For example, if your commercial database shows that textiles is a predominant industry, ask why their presentation shows that furniture manufacturers are the major industry.

Developing a Sales Plan

After you listen to all of the presentations, take the time to develop an annual sales plan to address the needs of the entire sales team. You won't be able to complete this during the first sixty days on the job (a good sales plan usually takes six to nine months to develop), but now is the time to begin the process. By starting to build a plan now, you will be ready to initiate improvement programs later.

At a minimum, your sales plan should include the following sections.

- *Current situation.* What is the current sales growth in the individual territories? What is the profile of key accounts? What industries do key customers represent? What is the mix of industries in each territory? What is the market potential in the district, and how does each territory compare in terms of market potential and market share? What is the volume of sales in each territory, by product? Who are the major competitors, and what is their market share?

- *Background.* Provide some background information that sheds light on the current performance of the territory. By knowing the cause of past problems and the reasons for past successes, your strategies will be better suited toward avoiding problems and maximizing opportunities in the future.

- *Strategy.* What direction do you want your sales team to pursue? Be careful to choose no more than three to four strategies (e.g., minimizing selling time on certain products, or generating additional leads from new sources), so that salespeople have a reasonable chance of achieving their goals.

- *Tactics.* These are the action steps that salespeople must take to achieve each strategy. For example, one tactic for minimizing selling time is to ask customers in remote locations to conduct demos for other prospects in the territory, so reps can reduce their travel time. Be sure to include time frames for each tactic.

- *Obstacles.* List those factors that are most likely to get in the way of implementing your strategies. Identify the steps that must be taken to overcome the obstacles.

- *Assumptions.* Every strategy is developed on the basis of certain assumptions regarding economic, intracompany, and competitive conditions, conditions that may change over time. You must identify your assumptions so that if conditions change, you can modify your strategies accordingly.

■ *Feedback mechanism.* Note in your plan how you will measure salespeople's progress toward accomplishing the strategies. The feedback mechanism could be a simple one-page monthly progress report to the group. (Note: this is separate from the feedback you give to each salesperson on their progress in meeting individual goals.)

Copies of your sales plan should be distributed to your sales team, your manager, and the director of marketing, for their comments and suggestions. Incorporate the best suggestions and make sure to modify the plan as needed, in responses to major market, customer, or internal changes.

Recruiting and Hiring

Another "people issue" you must address during the first sixty days in your new assignment is hiring. It's important that you develop a profile of the type of salesperson needed for your team, in case you have to fill an unexpected opening quickly (as discussed in Chapter 5). With this profile in hand, you can communicate your hiring criteria to recruiters. Following are some of the criteria to include.

■ *Assertiveness.* Depending on how competitive your marketplace is and how long the buying cycle, you will want to hire salespeople who are moderately to highly assertive. The shorter the buying cycle and the more competitive the marketplace, the more aggressive the salesperson will need to be.

■ *Ability to be a team player.* Project-oriented technical sales that involve a team approach require salespeople who can work well with other company personnel. The ability to be a team player is also important in nondirect selling activities, such as the setup of temporary teams to improve policies and create new sales strategies.

■ *Analytical skills.* If a salesperson is needed for a territory in which there are many customer problems, the person should have a good analytical mind, so that he or she can identify and resolve problems quickly and effectively. An analytical type is also required for territories that have been depressed for unknown reasons. In general, if a territory is considered a problem, for whatever reason, it's best to hire a problem-solver to work it.

- *Autonomy.* Make sure the people you hire have a high degree of autonomy. As noted in Chapter 3, today most salespeople must be capable of working independently, of taking initiative, and making their own decisions. Hiring people who are independent will also reinforce the environment of self-management and empowerment that is necessary to produce Total Quality Selling.

- *Territory development skills.* Before making any hiring decision, learn about the salesperson's ability to prospect and develop accounts into long-term business. Ask your recruit how many leads per month his or her territory received and of these leads, how many the rep developed.

Be aware that all salespeople will tell you that they prospect. It's good to get an outside confirmation of their skills in this area, if possible, by talking with the salesperson's previous sales manager (if this person is given as a reference). If you cannot make an independent confirmation of their track record, you can at least ask several penetrating questions to determine whether or not the rep really can perform to your expectations when it comes to territory development.

Now that you know your hiring requirements and have determined the questions to ask, it's time to start recruiting. Start looking for candidates early in your assignment by contacting two or three executive search firms, as discussed in Chapter 5. When an opening arises, your early recruiting efforts will result in your having a number of qualified recruits in the pipeline, waiting to be hired.

Administrative Issues

The final issue you'll have to deal with sometime in the first sixty days of your new assignment is paperwork. Unless your sales force is equipped with computers, make certain you proceed cautiously when doling out administrative tasks to salespeople.

Top performers invariably hate paperwork, whereas below-average performers seem not to care one way or the other. The top performers' chief complaints are that paperwork takes time that could be better spent selling and that excessive paperwork is like having Big Brother looking over their shoulders. Average to below-average performers, however, often see completed paper-work as evidence that they're hard at work and that their jobs are secure.

You can help matters by telling salespeople up front why you need, and how you will use, every piece of paperwork you request. (If it's because upper management demands it and you haven't yet been able to change this, tell your salespeople that.) At the same time, let them know that it's sales results, not completed paperwork, that will lead them to success.

At a minimum, you should require your reps to complete Daily Contact Reports, such as those described in Chapter 4. These reports are extremely useful in sales forecasting, building customer databases, and establishing market and competitor profiles, in addition to their value in monitoring sales activity.

Whatever reports you have your sales reps turn in, keep in mind that paperwork should always support sales goals. Pile on too much of it, and your salespeople will be unsure of your priorities. Worse, they may begin to equate activity (filling out forms) with productivity—a trap you want to avoid.

The First Ninety Days

During the first ninety days on the job, you must continue to monitor your reps' performance and offer them coaching as needed. You must also continue to develop your sales plan. And it's time to take on a few more tasks.

Determining Motivation

Within your first ninety days on the job, you must lay the groundwork for long-term motivation as well as for the short-term sprint. Knowing your people is a start—being aware of their knowledge, skills, and attitudes will get you over the initial hurdles. But determining what will motivate them for long-distance running goes far beyond first impressions.

How do you find out what motivates salespeople? There are any number of psychological models that managers can refer to, such as Maslow's "hierarchy of needs," but my advice is to use these models sparingly. I'd advise a more personal, practical approach: simply question and observe your salespeople, as discussed in Chapter 2.

For instance, at an appropriate time during your first few trips with your salespeople, ask them what they take the most pride in. Some will respond in terms of sales numbers; others will focus on getting that big order, the process of getting the order, beating the competition, or completing a lengthy government proposal. Still others will say they're motivated to be among the top five performers—or simply to be the best.

You'll find that money isn't always the primary motivator, but recognition is high on the list. Rookies want to be patted on the back, and even veteran salespeople want to know their standing among their peers. Recognition as a top performer is often what turns these pros on.

Your job as a sales manager is to discover each salesperson's source of internal motivation and make sure that it's directed toward the appropriate goals. One caution: motivation changes over time, so make sure that you question and monitor your salespeople's motivation every few months, or whenever a major personal or corporate event takes place.

Progressive Goal Management

During your first ninety days, you want to proceed with implementation of the Progressive Goal Management system outlined in Chapter 3. Select three to five salespeople from your district to serve on a focus group to critique the system and suggest modifications, as discussed in Chapter 3. By soliciting the input of a select group of salespeople before implementing the system, you ensure a higher level of acceptance and fewer implementation problems.

Once your focus group has disbanded, meet and discuss the proposed PGM system with every salesperson who was not in the focus group. As a result of the focus group, you should be ready with answers to potential objections to the system. Listen to objections with an open mind and be prepared to incorporate the best suggestions into the system.

When you discuss the PGM system, let each salesperson know that excellence in goal writing takes time and effort. Reassure them that their investment in the system will yield substantial rewards in terms of improved performance and (more importantly, from their point of view) higher sales commissions.

To make goal-writing fun rather than a chore, hold a one-time contest when you implement the system. Offer a cash prize or a trip to the salesperson who comes up with the best set of written goals on the first try. Consider having your manager and possibly your manager's manager on the panel of judges. This will give the issue of goal-setting high visibility.

The First 120 Days

The Move to Total Quality Selling

At this point you have laid the groundwork for a Total Quality Selling environment. You have travelled with your reps, have seen them in action, and have found out what motivates them. You have made your expectations clear and have established a high level of trust and credibility. You have implemented a Progressive Goal Management system. You are continuing to monitor your reps' performance, and to provide feedback and coaching. Your recruiting effort is in place. And you should be well on your way to completing your sales plan. Now it's time to let your salespeople know that you want them to make quality and continuous improvement a way of life.

In Chapter 7, we outlined the step-by-step process of customer-focused selling. Now is the time to coach your salespeople in this approach. As in the implementation of the Progressive Goal Management system, introduce the idea of quality selling to a select group of salespeople first. As your salespeople develop the skills of customer-focused selling, you will have to act as Quality Control manager, guiding your salespeople, monitoring and rewarding customer-focused behavior, using the techniques outlined in Chapter 6.

In Chapter 6, I noted the importance of senior management commitment in establishing and maintaining a total quality environment. Before you start on your journey to Total Quality Selling, enlist the support of the senior executives in your company. Among other things, that includes funding for outside training and the appropriate rewards to recognize those salespeople showing the highest level of quality improvement.

Most importantly, in striving to move your sales force in the direction of Total Quality Selling, make sure that you demonstrate the quality behaviors and attitudes that you expect your reps to adopt. Unless you lead by your own example, your salespeople will view your push toward quality as just another fad.

Note

1. The bulk of this section, "The First Sixty Days" and "The First Ninety Days," is adapted from Joseph A. Petrone, "The First 90 Days," *Sales & Marketing Management*, September 1992: 66. Reprinted by permission of *Sales & Marketing Management*. Copyright September 1992.

Index